"COMMUNIST AMERICA: MUST IT BE?"
MID-EIGHTIES UPDATE

"COMMUNIST AMERICA: MUST IT BE?"

MID-EIGHTIES UPDATE

By
Billy James Hargis
P.O. Box 977
Tulsa, Oklahoma 74102

New Leaf Press
P.O. BOX 311, GREEN FOREST, AR 72638

FIRST EDITION, 1986
25,000 Copies

Typesetting by SPACE
Berryville, AR 72616

Library of Congress Number: Applied For
ISBN Number: 0-89221-134-2

TABLE OF CONTENTS

DEDICATED TO:

H.J. Casey
State of Oregon

Whose love of the first book I wrote with this title in *1960,* and whose generous contribution underwrote the three years of research and preparation of this all-new "update" version.

INTRODUCTION

Some years ago I wrote a book called *Communist America, Must It Be?* that probably sold over a million copies because so many of the predictions in it became true within so short a time after it came off the press. These included the rapid expansion of Soviet aggression throughout the world; a sharp turn to the left in Washington policies and thinking; the decline and fall of public education in America with the end of prayer and Bible reading and the start of sex and drug education in the schools; the introduction of Marxism into American church life through the World and National Councils of Churches, and many other radical changes in America that today seem commonplace.

This book is an update of that one, some 30 years or so later. If anything, the situation has become worse instead of better since then. Communism has taken over Southeast Asia, vast areas of Africa and has strong footholds in the Western Hemisphere in Cuba and Nicaragua with revolution being exported from those countries with Soviet aid to El Salvador and other parts of Latin America. Education is worse than ever. The National Commission on Excellence in Education has said the mediocre public schools are a "risk" to America. Dozens of church denominations have split as liberal churchmen have, with the help of the communist-oriented WCC and NCC, tried to cast doubt on the inerrancy of the Bible, the virgin birth of Christ, the resurrection of Christ and nearly all of God's miracles both ancient and modern.

For these reasons and others, I believed it was time to update

7

Communist America, Must It Be? with this new book that is even more urgent than ever. There must never be a "communist America" but if it is to be prevented, Americans must know more about communism and its tactics and strategies than at anytime before. Communism has a way of lulling people into a false sense of security, into an "it can't happen here" way of thinking, into a communist state of mind subconsciously with the acceptance of socialism while denying communism on the surface.

Communists have taken advantage of this to install and entrench themselves into the American government bureaucracy while at the same time bringing communist revolution into this hemisphere and right to our doorstep with dire developments in Mexico and Central America.

The liberal national news media has made it fashionable to dismiss anti-communists as radicals themselves, as "right wing fanatics," as "nuts" and "oddballs" and other unflattering names. The news rarely has any anti-communist content and communists are most often referred to as "leftists" without being called what they are: communists. The news media has accepted the communist propaganda that communist revolutions are not communist at all but "liberation movements" or "people's uprisings" when in fact they are planned in the Kremlin and armed and supplied and financed by the Soviet Union.

The evidence of the communist threat to America is more than abundant. It is overwhelming and this book presents this evidence in an orderly and straightforward way that anyone can easily understand. We believe that every American should have an opportunity to read this book and understand it. That's why we have written it, to further fulfill the belief that I am serving God as an American "Watchman on the Wall" as it says in Ezekiel. I believe that among the readers of this book there will be patriotic Americans willing to take action and become leaders in the Christian Crusade for Christ and against communism.

As we survey the situation America is in today, we find not only a distressing decline of morality and patriotism within the nation but an alarming encirclement by communism on our borders and shores.

I am grateful to my colleague and Editor of Christian Crusade Newspaper, Bill Sampson, for assisting me in the writing of this book.

BILLY JAMES HARGIS
POST OFFICE BOX 977
TULSA, OKLAHOMA 94102

Chapter 1

WHAT'S WRONG WITH AMERICA?

America is still the greatest country on earth, or as we like to say it, the greatest country under the living Son. But it won't be long if the forces of Satan, led by communism and aided and abetted by greed, corruption and immorality have their way. These forces cannot be defeated by any means of man but only by God. Americans must know about these forces in order to identify them, isolate them and seek God's grace through prayer and faith to destroy them.

America is still a country of a Christian majority living Christian lives and trying to be an example to the rest of the world in decency and civilization. But Satan's forces, too often praised and glorified by a decadent national news media, are at work against the very principles of Christianity, decency and civilization which make this country great.

If we had to put America's troubles into a nutshell we would say it is financially broke, educationally corrupted and spiritually declining.

Here are the facts:

FAILURE OF THE FINANCIAL SYSTEM

America has a one-way ticket aboard the poorhouse express because we cannot or will not stop financing communism. From 1946 to the mid-1980s we have spent $290 billion on foreign economic and military assistance, loans by American banks that have not been paid back and grants to the United Nations' International Monetary Fund, the World Bank and the Export-Import Bank.

Many billions of dollars of this money has gone to Communist Russia, Communist Poland, Communist Romania, Communist Yugoslavia and now Communist China is in line for a big handout.

Much of this financial chicanery has been disguised by "laundering" American taxpayer money through the UN's International Monetary Fund and World Bank, making it look like the United States is supporting world peace in the name of the United Nations when in fact the money is funneled around in a confusing flow only to wind up in the hands of communists.

Here are the financial details:

•Compounding the interest on "foreign aid" both public and private provided by American taxpayers, workers and investors, the American economy has been sapped...and that's a good word for it...of **$2 trillion, 304 billion dollars**. This figure is so incomprehensible that we have chosen to spell it out. In numerals it is the figure two followed by so many zeros, along with "304" thrown in just left of center, that the characters would appear more the result of a stuck typesetting computer than anything with real meaning.

•The entire national debt is only $1 trillion dollars, less than half of what has been sent overseas to finance the industrial buildup of our competitive trading allies and the military buildup of our enemies. With the government adding an annual budget deficit of $200 billion on top of that, the national debt will be $3 trillion by the year 2,000 and at the present rate the foreign aid figure will be $6 trillion dollars.

(NOTE: *A trillion is one million, million dollars. Consider it this way...if you set out to count one million dollars, one dollar at a time, in a 12-hour day, 7-day week you would require 24 days without lunch or coffee breaks. To count a billion in the same manner you would work 64 years. To count a trillion you would require 64,000 years. To count what we have given in foreign aid in that manner would require 147 thousand, two hundred and ninety six years. But take heart! A computer counting at the speed of 186,000 per second and working around the clock could do it in just 9 years, 4 months and 4 days. Perhaps we should require our congressmen to count everything they give away one at a time.)*

•Since 1946 the U.S. government has given the UN's World Bank $8.5 billion and an additional $12.8 billion gift to the bank from the U.S. taxpayer has been authorized to be paid out of the 1985 fiscal year. **These dollars are headed mostly for communists, bankrupts, deadbeats, freeloaders and insolvent countries.**

10

• Mexico, where communists run the bureaucracy and long ago corrupted the government, is in the process of receiving $1 billion in American bank loans and $4.5 billion in International Monetary Fund credits, **20 per cent of which is directly from the American taxpayers pockets.**

• Brazil, some $100 billion in the red, partly from having built a completely impractical new "capital city" called Brasilia in the remote jungles of the Amazon Basin, recently received a $1.2 billion "loan" from the U.S. Treasury to tide it over until an additional $6 billion loan is completed through the International Monetary Fund. Incidentally, the new city of Brasilia has become a cropper with no new businesses or industries wanting to move to the remote location and some government offices having already moved back to Rio de Janeiro and Sao Paulo. All this while Brazil is enjoying a bonanza gold strike!

• **Marxist Zimbabwe has received U.S. government guaranteed loans, gifts and pledges of more than $300 million, PROVING THAT TERRORISM PAYS!**

• Marxist Nicaragua got a $34 million "loan" from the World Bank subsidiary known as the Inter-American Development Bank, prompting Ron Paul of Texas to say:

"Americans are forced to pay for these international lending institutions with their tax dollars, and then they get hit a second time with skyrocketing interest rates as a result of so much money going overseas and making it scarce here at home."

• At the end of 1983, Congress and the President approved a controversial $5.8 billion "emergency" contribution to the UN's International Monetary Fund, America's part of a $32.5 billion IMF package designed largely to be given to debtor countries so it can be paid back to international banks as interest on loans to the deadbeats. **This means that taxpayers are being sacrificed to the poorhouse so big banks that made stupid loans won't have to go there.**

• Nigeria, where a military regime overthrew a mockery of a so-called "democratic government" early in 1984, is another country that built a new "capital city" miles inland from its major port of Lagos and now owes billions of dollars to bankers and U.S. taxpayers that never will be repaid. Despite its oil business, Nigeria is among the top 10 debtor countries of the world and can barely make interest payments on what it owes.

• Upper Volta, one of Africa's poorest countries, has people barefoot, in rags and starving, while its striped-pants and top-hatted delegation to the United Nations begs money from the

11

IMF and World Bank during the day, then lives it up at night in some of the fanciest New York City restaurants, night clubs and hotels.

•Communist China is in the process of receiving $2 billion a year (a year!) from the UN's World Bank, with 20 per cent of it being paid by U.S. taxpayers.

•So far as the Soviet Union is concerned, the United States continues to send a massive flow of military and industrial technology to the communist rulers of Russia, along with guaranteed loans, cash loans and outright tax dollars. **This means that American taxpayers must pay for the entire arms race, both the Soviet military buildup and the American response to it!**

•Communist China's alleged "opening up to U.S. trade" is nothing more than a political and news media smokescreen to hide the fact that the communists in Peking are next in line to get the same free technology and financial deal that Moscow has been getting for years. Red China will have been in the United Nations long enough by 1986 to be eligible for loans from the U.N. World Bank and International Monetary Fund. The Chinese Communists plan to soak American taxpayers for billions of dollars through U.N.-sponsored "loans" that will never be repaid. We have said all along that the split between Moscow and Peking was phony, staged to fool the United States into thinking it could use Red China as a buffer or a counter-weight of some kind against the Soviet Union. Now that Red China has conned the United States into all kinds of agreements for economic aid and nuclear power plants and cooling off our friendship with the real China on Taiwan, the Red Chinese and the Red Russians are getting real friendly themselves—two communist superpowers preparing to unite against the United States and the rest of the free World.

Here is what is going on:

As soon as President Reagan got out of Peking, the first deputy chairman of the Soviet Council of Ministers arrived right on his heels. Now the Soviet Union and Red China have reached agreements to expand trade, to increase cultural exchanges, and — most important — to jointly build Communist China's two largest plants, a steel mill and a nuclear power plant. What with both the Soviet Union and Red China getting money from the United States through favorable trade deals and outright foreign aid, Uncle Sam is the one most likely to foot the bill for the Red China steel mill and nuclear plant...with the Soviet Union getting the credit.

The Red superpowers are talking about three things bothering Red China: the Soviet military presence on the Chinese and Mongolian borders, the Soviet troops in Afghanistan and Moscow's support of the Vietnamese occupation of Cambodia. All that is **smokescreen stuff for news media consumption.** The troops on the border are to fool the United States into thinking there is still a rift or division between the two Red superpowers. As for the murder and aggression in Afghanistan and Cambodia, the communists in China could care less. They have done the same thing in Manchuria and Korea and Tibet and Mongolia. **The communists are all blood brothers when it comes to murder.**

All the alleged points of disagreement are so much communist propaganda. Another thing they did was announce a "non-nuclear zone" along the Soviet borders with Mongolia and Red China. This is intended for public consumption worldwide to show how peaceful these two Red gangsters are and to try to embarrass the United States before world opinion into a "nuclear freeze." The Soviet Union and Red China are using this phony "non-nuclear zone" as an alleged example that they have peaceful intentions...an example they expect the United States to follow by agreeing to a nuclear freeze which would then leave the Soviets with **nuclear superiority!**

They are simply trying to **blackmail the United States** through world opinion. What worries Moscow most is the deployment of new U.S. medium-range missiles in Western European countries in response to the Soviet's original placement of such missiles within range of Western Europe. They don't like the idea of the free world trying to defend itself against communism.

Meanwhile, Red China is moving in the late 1980s to get the U.S. to finance the modernization of China—and its military might—just as we have the Soviet Union's since World War II.

America's continued financing of communists and Latin American deadbeats has bankrupted the country. We live with a huge national debt and an annual federal budget deficit. We have a financial system made out of paper money and stuck together with chicken wire and chewing gum, also known as the "faith and credit of the American people." It won't take much of a bad financial wind to blow the flimsy structure down as America approaches the brink of financial disaster. Big banks are in even more hot water with their shareholders and depositors.

Not long ago Bolivia failed to make a payment on interest of its debt for the third straight month, which automatically puts

13

it in the deadbeat debtor class along with a bunch of other communist and Latin American countries who are still sucking money out of the American taxpayers through the funnel of the International Monetary Funds, the United Nations' agency supported mostly by the United States.

Wall Street stockbrokers are talking backwards like they usually do about troubled businesses. Instead of saying the big banks are in big trouble, they are ballyhooing how "cheap" bank stocks are and what good buys they are for such low prices.

I don't know how many people will be fooled into buying big bank shares at alleged bargain prices, but I do know why they are so cheap—it's because the banks are swamped with bad loans they can't even collect the interest on, to say nothing of the principal, and the people who own shares in those banks are trying to unload them at almost any price they can get for them.

The shares of nine of the largest American banks have gone down drastically.

Bank of America, $16.25 a share, **down 35 per cent** from its 1983-1984 high; Banker's Trust, $38.50, **down 24 per cent;** Chase Manhattan, the David Rockefeller Bank, $39.75, **down 35 per cent;** Chemical Bank of New York (adjusted for a share split during the period), $24.13, **down 33 per cent;** Citicorp of New York, which is Chase Manhattan's "cousin" in banking, $28.87, **down 33 per cent;** Continental Illinois, bailed out by the Federal Deposit Insurance Corporation, $5.50, **down a whopping 78 per cent;** Manufacturer's Hanover, known as "Manny Hanny" in the banking game, $26.37, **down 45 per cent;** J.P. Morgan Bank, $64, **down 19 per cent;** First Chicago, $21.00, **down 25 per cent.**

Financial consultant Goldman, Sachs recommends that the public steer clear of any bank shares of banks with large Latin loans.

The J.P. Morgan Bank and Texas Commerce Bancshares are the only two major American banks that still have a Triple-A rating from Standard & Poors!

The banks are largely to blame for their own greed, making stupid loans to poor countries and communist countries who can't even pay back interest. But the Federal Reserve, the privately-owned money controller which doesn't have to answer to Congress or the President or apparently to anyone, is also to blame for simply authorizing the **printing of more and more paper money** for these stupid banks to cover up their bad books and dumb investments. But the payoff is approaching and some of these banks face failure unless they extend these bad loans far into the 21st Century and the Federal Reserve supplies even more tons of worthless paper money for them to circulate and cover-up their mistakes.

Some people believe in banks more than they believe in God...at least they put more of their money into banks than into God's work. In reading the news pages and financial sheets, I haven't read yet that God is failing...only the big banks.

A scandal of gigantic proportions is building within the American banking system and the three regulatory agencies that supposedly control it—the Federal Reserve, the U.S. Office of the Comptroller, and the Federal Deposit Insurance Corporation.

The scandal is that the supposed regulatory agencies have now joined the big banks in a gigantic financial gamble to keep the banks from failing because of bad loans made to communist and Third World countries, when their duty is to regulate them.

There have been major bank failures and near failures recently, marked by colossal mismanagement, insider self-dealing loans to bank directors and bank managers, expansion of long-term loans on the basis of short-term borrowing, the use of volatile and unstable fund sources to support illiquid and high-risk asset portfolios, overnight borrowings from bank to bank to an unsafe degree to fund forward loan commitments.

These are just a few of the scandalous goings on behind the scenes in banking and the supposed regulatory agencies not only have failed to enforce regulations, they are now instead joining the banks in high-risk gambles by investing public money in them and side-stepping banking laws to help banks gamble unstead of cracking down on them.

The Federal Reserve is the worst offender. In the Franklin National Bank failure, the Federal Reserve had advanced $1.5 BILLION in what were technically public funds, your money and mine, to try to save the bank but all was lost. The Federal Reserve just printed up another $1.5 billion to replace it...$1.5 billion with nothing backing it but our faith and credit. The public interest of America is not being served by this practice of the Federal Reserve to underwrite the illiquidity and insolvency of banks in circumstances characterized by recent large bank failures...and there will be more.

Not to be outdone by the Federal Reserve, the Federal Deposit Insurance Corporation has plunged into a $2 billion fund with a consortium of banks to try to save Continental Illinois National Bank and Trust Co. from collapse. The regulators have become banks themselves, lenders of last resort, relying upon not only the taxpayers money, as in the case of the Federal Reserve, but now on the money of depositors in **ALL** banks, in **OTHER** banks, to bail out troubled banks, as in the case of the FDIC and Continental Illinois.

This scandal is happening because bankers have been able to play the fragmented regulatory structure, shifting back and forth from one to another . . . whichever one they thought would best accommodate their views. And now they are **pulling the regulators down** into the **financial quicksand** with them. There is financial disaster ahead in banking if something isn't done. And it could **cost you** everything you have in the bank.

Here is what should be done. Congress, which created the independent and privately-owned Federal Reserve, should abolish it, along with the Federal Reserve Insurance Corporation and the Comptroller of the Currency as bank regulators. All have covered themselves with **shame and complicity** in this growing bank scandal.

Not only are dozens of big American banks in financial trouble because of bad loans to communist and "Third World" countries, they are starting to pull the Federal Reserve and Federal Deposit Insurance Corporation into the quicksand with them.

Our Banks Are In Trouble

America's biggest banks are in trouble—they have been bailed out twice within the last few years by American taxpayers through the International Monetary Fund, which is the United Nations' bank. American taxpayers pay for most of the U.N. budget, including the International Monetary Fund.

. Chase Manhattan, the Rockefeller bank, and its New York look-alike, Citibank of New York, have loaned out billions they can't get back to lthe likes of Poland, Argentina, Brazil, Mexico and dozens of communist-controlled African nations. They keep tapping the International Monetary Fund for help, which in turn taps the Federal Reserve, which in turn taps the U.S. Treasury, which in turn taps the taxpayers.

America's seventh-largest bank has fallen into the financial mess with them: Continental Illinois National Bank and Trust Co. of Chicago. It made incredibly stupid loans through the failed Penn Square Bank in Oklahoma City to a wide-range of oilmen promising get-rich-quick schemes then the bottom fell out of the oil business. Continental depositors ran on the bank in 1984 and pulled out more than $4 billion in deposits.

A scheme to put all American depositors behind the failing bank was developed in which the Federal Deposit Insurance Corporation, The FDIC — not to be confused with the Federal Reserve — for the first time in its history provided $2 billion in additional capital along with commercial banks in the form of subordinated notes to bail out Continental.

The big bankers now have grabbed hold of the FDIC that insures your deposits in banks up to $100,000. The FDIC is underwriting some $4.5 billion for just this one Chicago bank...and that puts your personal bank deposits in jeopardy along with Continental, the bank that went through a $4 billion run on its deposits by people who don't trust it anymore. Now you have to trust it through the FDIC whether you like it or not.

With the Federal Deposit Insurance Corporation gambling on Continental, there are no more guaranteed, sure-thing investments anymore, least of all in banks, once the supposed backbone of American finance.

The privately-owned Federal Reserve is busy printing up tons of paper money night and day to keep the banks from failing. That's why we have high interest rates. The government can't control its spending. That's another reason why we have high interest rates. Now the FDIC is in the **gambling game with banks.**

More banks and other financial institutions are going to fail in the near future as the world financial crisis continues. The banks have brought this trouble upon themselves.

The public is losing confidence in banks because of their poor management, bad loans, financial losses, exhorbitant service fees, expansion into other fields, monopoly-style branch banking and inexperienced personnel.

American banks are controlled by the privately-owned and unconstitutional **Federal Reserve System,** a misnamed creation of big international one-world bankers who imposed it on a weak and naive Congress still shaken by the financial panic of 1907. Since then, the country has suffered its worst depressions and wars in the nation's history.

The Federal Reserve is merely a branch itself of the world's super central bank, the Bank for International Settlements in Basel, Switzerland, whose board dictates world financial policy. The Federal Reserve chairman attends the board meetings 10 times a year to receive instructions but is only an ex-officio and non-voting member who is usually called upon only to supply American dollars to the United Nations' International Monetary Fund and World Bank for loans and bailouts to Third World deadbeats and communist countries.

The laws and financial instruments developed since 1929 in an effort to avoid further financial crises and panics have proven inadequate in recent times as the world's financial troubles mount. The Federal Reserve is responsible for this because it has become nothing more than a tool of big, bad international banking. The Federal Reserve was given authority by Congress in 1913 to issue and control all American currency. It accepts bonds issued by the U.S. Treasury Department in exchange for currency and coin issues. The Federal Reserve and the Treasury have ruined the value of the American dollar by over-issuing it—bales and bales, carloads and carloads of paper money.

The supposed high value of the American dollar against other national currencies in 1984-85 only revealed that the other currencies are in even worse shape, also having been over-issued without any substantial backing.

The world debt is actually an American debt. It is being floated and expanded by the withholding tax on American wages which underwrites the issuance of U.S. bonds to the bank-owned Federal Reserve in exchange for Federal Reserve Notes which now pass as American currency. The banks which control it have siphoned billions of dollars into bad loans to such losers as Brazil ($100 billion in debt), Argentina ($43.6 billion in debt) and Mexico ($87 billion in debt) along with billions to communist-bloc countries and their so-called "Third World" allies.

The siphon used to transfer these funds from the American worker to the deadbeats and communists is the United Nations' International Monetary Fund and World Bank. The *killer loan* that could break all the banks will be made in 1986 when Red China becomes eligible for IMF and World Bank loans. The money will come from American taxpayers.

It is these billions in bad loans that have caused American banks to charge exhorbitant service fees for what used to be free or relatively inexpensive financial charges. The banks are now milking their customers for everything they can get to stave off the *financial disaster* caused by the loss of multi-billions in bad loans.

The increase in these service fees from 1979 to 1985 included the following:

1. **A per check charge hike from 10 cents to 13 cents.**

18

2. Monthly maintenance fee of accounts raised from $1.17 to $2.51.

3. Stop payment service on checks increased from $3.15 to $7.28.

4. Safe deposit box rentals up from $7.06 to $11.37.

5. Bounced check penalty hiked from $5.07 to $9.46.

6. Minimum balance for free checking raised from $286 to $429.

7. Percentage of banks charging for checking, up from 81.5 per cent to 94.7 per cent.

In addition to these routine customer gougings, banks collectively are making about $60 billion a year in interest off check floats. If you receive an insurance check, a securities sales check, or, in the case of college students for example, even a check from home for expenses, you may have to wait as long as 10 days to three weeks for the check to clear an out-of-town bank or financial institution before the money will be available to you. This is totally ridiculous in the age of instant computer communications but it means the banks get to use your money, loaning it out for interest you will never receive, during the period the check is supposedly being "cleared" out-of-town. In reality, the check can be cleared in minutes by computer systems but banks, prefer to use your money without paying you for it.

Despite their customer gouging and profiteering, bank failures and so-called "problem banks" are on the rise. There were some 70 bank failures in 1984 compared with 45 in 1983, 40 in 1982, and only 10 or fewer from 1981 back through 1977. More than 100 are expected to fail in 1985 and 1986.

"Problem banks" are another matter. The Federal Reserve says there are at least 800 problem banks. . .banks that are in a serious enough financial condition that they are tottering on the edge of bankruptcy or rapidly approaching that status. But depositors of those banks don't know their bank is in trouble because the Federal Reserve is not a federal agency but is privately-owned and is not under obligation to announce to the public what banks are problem banks. That means when they fail, investors and depositors get stuck and have to rely on the Federal Deposit Insurance Corporation to get their money back.

But now the FDIC has changed drastically and if its new policy continues it could find itself in deep financial trouble. This came about with the unprecedented $4.5 billion bailout of Chicago's Continental Illinois Bank, resulting in the forced resignations of 10 Continental directors, obviously for mismanagement. There is only $17 billion in the FDIC's insurance fund and with some 800 banks on the "problem" list, banking insiders question whether the FDIC can insure depositors, having used nearly a third of that amount to bail out Continental alone.

Despite the Federal Reserve's secrecy concerning problem banks, it is obvious that certain big banks are having serious problems whether they are on the problem list or not. Some of the loses banks have suffered recently have been staggering and yet they go on losing, believing now that the FDIC will bail them out as it did Continental. FDIC "insurance" is nothing more than money allocated to it from taxpayer funds.

It is the working American taxpayer who is being forced to shoulder the load now for American banking follies and mistakes.

Spectacular Losses

Some of the recent spectacular banking losses have been by First Chicago, losing $72 million in the third quarter of 1983, largely on defaulted farm loans; the Oklahoma City Penn Square failure caused the Continental Illinois loss which in turn cost the Rockefellers' Chase Manhattan, third largest U.S. bank, a $200 million loss; Manufacturers Hanover of New York's third quarter 1983 earnings were down 23 per cent; Chase Manhattan's third quarters earnings were down 38 per cent and New York Citicorp's third quarter earnings fell 14 per cent.

Citicorp is typical of arrogant big bank attitudes that deceive people through their statements in the news media. John Reed, the new Citicorp chairman, was quoted in the media as having said: "I think the banking industry is perfectly capable of meeting the needs of society. We are part of society and we are decent people."

The "*decent people*" of Citicorp, in addition to a 13 per cent decline in earnings for its investors in third-quarter 1983, recently tried to force its poorer depositors, those with less than $5,000 in their accounts, to use only automatic transfer machines so live tellers could devote their time to more affluent customers. While relegating its poorer customers to machines only, the "*decent people*" at Citicorp have instituted free money management programs for its customers who have $25,000 or more on account, eliminated waiting lines for them and virtually showers them with personal attention. That's decency, banker style.

Other *"decent people"* in the banking industry include Houston Medical Center Bank which ignores the poor completely and accepts only doctors and other wealthy people as customers, loaning them the bank's airplane, providing limousine service and theater ticket acquisition. It seems, despite Mr. Reed's claim, that many banks are *"decent"* only to the more wealthy among their customers.

Confidence and Loans Lost

It is little wonder that the American Banker newspaper reported recently that a survey it financed revealed that 36 per cent of those polled said their confidence in banks had failed. A Gallup poll showed that the percentage of Americans who profess a high degree of faith in bankers declined from 60 per cent in 1979 to 51 per cent in 1984.

It is foreign loans, many of them hopelessly lost, totalling $350 billion that have the banks in their most serious trouble. Most of their executives responsible for bad loans were fools, and greedy fools at that.

S.C. Gwynne, a former loan officer for what he would describe only as a "medium-sized Midwestern bank" revealed in a recent Harper's magazine article that when he visited the Philippines in 1978 to make a loan to a major construction company with a government contract he was loaned a red Jaguar automobile and "a pretty 20-year-old woman." He commented that on a loan journey to Thailand he was loaned a silver Lincoln auto but no woman. His bank loaned the Philippine firm $10 million on the basis of the government contract but it failed to meet its loan repayments.

McNamara's Bad Advice

Many banks got in trouble as they followed the advice of Robert Strange McNamara, now a past president of the U.N.'s World Bank, to recycle petroleum wealth from the rich to the needy my making huge loans to the "Third World." Now McNamara is gone and the banks are stuck with their bad loans made on his advice.

During the McNamara stampede to make unsecured loans to foreign governments and other foreign borrowers, some bankers were so anxious to get in on the action that while they were away from their office during lunch hours they empowered their secretaries to promise $5 million to $10 million as part of any loan package for the likes of Brazil and Mexico, now the world's top two debtor nations.

And yet, despite all these self-inflicted wounds, the big

21

banks continue to make bad loans to developing countries that have no prospect for repaying them. A Morgan Guaranty economist projects that such loans will increase to 5 per cent annually during the next few years!

Fed Encouraged Flops

Many bankers are saying, in their defense, that they were encouraged to make the bad loans by the Federal Reserve and the U.S. Treasury Department. The Treasury and the Fed are joints in the siphon also comprised of the IMF and World Bank and Bank for International Settlements to transfer wealth from American wage earners via the withholding tax into the international banking funnel that conducts it to communists and deadbeats overseas with no prospects of repayment.

Such loans, underwritten by the taxpayer, are merely tacked on to the far end of the ever-growing national debt now amounting to a $200 billion a year federal deficit and a total $1.4 trillion and rising national debt.

Oklahoma Congressman Mickey Edwards takes a dim view of the federal deficit, saying: "There is no way you or I will ever see a balanced budget in our lifetime."

The reason is that the government has lost control of America's financial destiny. No one, not the President or the Congress or the Treasury Department, can do anything realistically about the drain of U.S. taxpayers' money into the international banking system or cartel, not since 1913 when the Federal Reserve was handed the power by Congress, unconstitutionally, to issue currency.

The Fed has done so with a vengeance, printing billions and billions of paper dollars with nothing of substance to back them but "the faith and credit" of the federal government, meaning the U.S. taxpayer, who is starting to lose faith and has precious little credit standing anymore, especially if he is only a small saver and not a $100,000 account eligible for the use of bank airplanes and limousines and inside money management.

Americans Duped

Speaking of credit, we wrote in one of our recent books, *The Federal Reserve Scandal,* under heading of "Suckers Pay," that "American bankers loaned infinitely and indiscriminately to nearly all comers throughout the world. The United Nations, through its International Monetary Fund and World Bank, was glad to give practically all U.N. members a good credit rating, if that's all it took, to transfer billions in wealth from the West and its hard-working industrialized nations, to the rest of the world.

"**Americans won't realize they have been duped into permanently higher interest rates and ever lasting debt and much lower currency value until the mid-1980s and later.**"

Congressman Edwards' statement was an early indication that the realization is beginning to dawn on some people who have examined the approaching financial disaster and the history behind it.

Time Magazine recently reported: "For the moment, the world economic recovery has improved the financial prospects of debtor nations by helping them boost exports. In addition, falling interest rates and increased aid from the International Monetary Fund have eased their debt burden. But no one is convinced that the foreign-loan problem has been solved. Bankers recognize that an upsurge in interest rates or a U.S. recession could ignite the debt troubles once again."

Time **writes blithely of the International Monetary Fund as though it were some kind of manna from heaven. The truth is, although *Time* failed to mention it, is that the IMF gets most of its money from the United States, meaning the U.S. taxpayer.**

Understand this: the federal deficit and the world debt, practically all of it in American money loaned out to foreigners, will not be repaid to U.S. taxpayers if repaid at all. The fact is that we don't "owe it to ourselves," meaning the federal deficit, as the now discredited economist John Maynard Keynes once told the news media, but owe it to international bankers who have siphoned it out of us for use as they have seen fit, use decided in secret at board meetings of the Bank for International Settlements, use dictated without democratic process or representation. Its the old story: taxation without representation.

WHEN BANKS COLLAPSE

When the big banks of New York that have made foolish loans to foreign deadbeats and communists collapse, the American taxpayer should not be inside them handing money to the bankers.

If bankers David Rockefeller of Chase Manhattan and John Reed of Citicorp (and his predecessor, banking "genius" Walter Wriston) and other would-be financial wizards who are on the verge of going under soon haven't learned anything about their stupid loans, certainly the American taxpayer should have learned by now.

The 1983-84 $8.4 billion bailout of the big banks by providing the deadbeats and communists with enough money to pay interest on their loans for a short time is proving to be a complete disaster, just as many said it would.

When Rockefeller, Wriston-Reed, and Rockefeller's "international adviser" Henry Kissinger lobbied the bailout through the U.S. Congress on behalf of the United Nations' International Monetary Fund, they promised to impose "austerity" on the borrowing countries such as Mexico, Brazil and Argentina, meaning those countries must produce more and buy less from the United States.

The trouble is that they are not producing more but demanding more loans, and they are indeed not buying as much from the U.S., causing American unemployment increases and declining production. The communists are telling the Latin Americans that the "austerity program" imposed by the International Monetary Fund is nothing but the "Yankees' Banks' Collection Agency."

A senior vice president of Citicorp recently said: **"Let's tell the truth. Nobody's debts are going to be repaid."**

And Robert McNamara, former head of the World Bank who engineered many of the now bad loans that transfered billions from the American economy into Third World and communist nations, said recently: **"A commercial banker would be out of his mind to finance all of the external financial requirements of India and China and he ought to be removed if he did."**

That's something, coming from McNamara, who promoted most of the financial trouble in the first place during his dozen years or so as head of the World Bank. He is referring to the fact that Red China will be eligible for World Bank loans in 1986 and a huge loan to the communists there will cause the predicted bank collapses.

While the U.S. prime rate hovers around 12 or 13 per cent, the World Bank is still loaning American capital to bankrupt governments abroad at 10 per cent! The World Bank recently loaned $590 million more to four Latin American countries and can hardly wait until Red China asks for a massive **bank-breaking loan** in 1986. That's the one that could cause world-wide financial chaos and another serious depression if it is made.

The new president of the World Bank is A.W. Clausen and he is making speeches on how "important" it is that Red China be loaned billions of dollars . . . those billions to be funneled from the American taxpayer into the U.N.'s World Bank by

24

way of Congress and then on to Red China.

This fiscal insanity, this continued financing of communists and other Yankee-hating deadbeats, has got to stop if America and freedom are to survive. Let the big banks collapse and take their beating as they deserve but there is no sense dragging the rest of us down with them by continued financing of their bad loans and interest.

America is not going to fail when those big banks collapse but it will fail if the American taxpayers are inside with all of our tax payments when the roofs of the banks fall in.

Chapter 2

FAILURE OF AMERICAN SCHOOLS

Not long before this book went to press, the U.S. Supreme Court dealt another drastic blow to American education, much as it did in the 1962-63 decisions banning prayer and Bible reading from the schools.

The high court ruled that homosexuals and lesbians can "advocate"---that is, teach---their "life style" in the classroom on grounds of freedom of speech. So we have come to this in American public education: kids can be taught homosexuality and lesbianism but they can't say a prayer or read the Bible! Oh God, forgive America for being so foolish!

The schools can teach sex education and drug education but they can't mention Jesus, His life or works.

The schools can teach Darwin's theory of evolution but they can't teach the Genesis account of creation.

The schools can teach Marxism but they can't teach the Ten Commandments.

The schools can teach Soviet history but they can't teach Bible history.

The schools can teach Castro but they can't teach Christ.

The schools can teach Lenin but they can't teach God.

The schools can teach communism but they can't teach Christianity.

The schools can teach everything that's wrong but they can't teach what the Bible says is right.

In short, American public education is in a mess. It is teaching future generations of Americans and is sealing the doom of this nation unless there are some immediate and drastic changes and improvements. But there is no sign such reform is coming. All "reform" seems to be based on the expenditure of more money, not on returning prayer and Bible reading and God to the classrooms of America.

Years after the Federal Commission on Education Excellence issued its reform recommendations, American schools are still receiving failing marks.

And they will continue to receive failing marks because the commission and other would-be reformers have all missed the point, which is the need of restoration of prayer and Bible reading in the public schools.

Until God's Word and spiritual recognition of the Supreme Being are put back into American classrooms, no amount of money, no amount of administrative tinkering, no amount of curriculum changes, no amount of rescheduling, no amount of merit pay, no amount of any and all other education reforms will improve the schools because none can do the job like God.

The report by the National Commission on Excellence in Education titled *A Nation at Risk* was issued in April, 1983, and said that the state of public school education in America nearly amounted to a state of "war" against the students because it was so poor. This caused a great stir and all manner of school reforms were discussed and some have been tried, most of them amounting to spending more money on schools that have fewer pupils than in the recent past. The news media have grasped at the few examples of improvement and given them considerable publicity, but on the whole, the schools are still failing and generally are worse off than they were when the report was issued despite the would-be reform efforts.

Why is this? Why can't the schools improve?

Here are the answers:

1. Despite all the reform efforts, the **humanist** grip on the schools is still too strong for educators, legislators and courts to overcome. Prayer and Bible reading has not been restored even though President Reagan has recommended it. He is not a dictator and can't order it done and the Congress, courts, educators and legislators have not been able to reject the humanist control of education, in favor of God. Unless and until this is done, the schools as a whole will never improve.

2. Educators generally took the commission's report as a personal insult. The education intellectuals, scholars, theorists, bureaucrats, administrators and far too many teachers became testy and aggressive in rejecting suggested reforms instead of cooperative.

3. Too many politicians and educators combined to change

the subject when true reforms were discussed, in effect, they said the schools were not that bad, that some programs were "first-rate," that education critics had personal or political motives, that the report was out-of-date before it was ever issued when schools were on the upgrade, and finally, that reformers were trying to "turn back the clock" and were "reactionary" and "ultra-conservative."

4. Too much blame and attention has been laid on the teachers. Suggestions for testing teacher competency, to scale them on merit pay, to re-educate or over-educate them diverted attention away from the real problem of what is basically wrong with public education, to wit, the greatest answer book in the world, the Bible, is banned from the schools along with morality.

5. The idea of philosophy that public schools are "democratic" and as a result all students must be "equal" and that poor students, even bad students, and academically crippled students must be somehow made to appear to be as good as bright and advanced students, still controls public education thinking.

6. The above reason, No. 5, has led educators to actually fear **excellence** in the schools. For example, in Ann Arbor, Michigan, home of the University of Michigan, the public school administrators in that city responded to the federal report by proposing a few modest increases in high school graduation requirements. The plan called for three years of math and science, requiring even marginal students to pass basic chemistry, geometry, algebra and logic to graduate. It meant eliminating some "electives" such as driver education, sex education, various career-oriented courses, certain art and athletic fringe courses and other activities long looked upon by students as relatively "easy" courses.

Teachers and principals protested, generally saying the plan was too simplistic, too reactionary. One principal said it resembled the curriculum of 20 years ago. There were claims of lack of consultation. There was a lot of education double-talk, such as the contention that the students didn't lack basic education as the reforms suggested but instead were passive, apathetic, thought linearally and were dependent too much on authority. It was anyone's guess what all that meant or what it had to do with education reform.

At any rate, the school administration backed down from the uproar and controversy and the reform plan was dropped.

The same thing happened in different details in school systems throughout the nation as the education modernists

triumphed over reformers who were cast into reactionary and simplistic roles and held up to scorn and ridicule by education "experts," meaning those resisting change in the system that places Darwin over God.

And through all of this is the undercurrent of racism, the feeling among many educators and within many communities that any reforms in public education would be to the disadvantage of racial minorities, that they would be "undemocratic" and that students would not be treated "equally."

This is the socialism of mankind at work as opposed to the true democracy of God. God is no respecter of persons as such and treats all equally who believe in Him. It is mankind that elevates one man or group of men, one person or group of persons, over others. It was Christ who offered equality and liberation to the poor, to women, to the downtrodden, to the unrecognized, not man. Yet the schools go on dictatorially claiming they are democratic while not recognizing God as the Great Equalizer. Perhaps the educators don't really want equality in the schools as they claim but want their own ranked "status quo."

One of the results of the turmoil in public education has been the tremendous increase in private school enrollments and the proliferating number of Christian schools. Parents of students in these schools continue to pay double taxation for education, financing the private schools and paying taxes for public schools their children no longer use. President Reagan's efforts to institute tax credits for private school tuition have been spurned by Congressional opponents.

Calls for public school parents to pay for their childrens' school lunches instead of having them tax subsidized, that they pay for band instruments and athletic gear and other incidental school expenses have been rejected by educators and legislators as undemocratic and reactionary.

Despite the financial burden of supporting two school systems, parents concerned about Christian education and quality education continue to turn away from godless and "modernist" public schools to support quality private schools and Christian schools. Millions of parents have become disillusioned and disgusted with public school education that teaches:

• Sex education emphasizing abortion and birth control without parental knowledge has led to record teen-age pregnancies.

• Drug education that has taught the many types of drugs

without halting their use among school-age children. (The recent book **Bad Blood** about the murder of two parents and the widespread drug abuse by teen-agers in Marin County, California, indicated that the teen drug situation is not geographically or socially limited in America.)

• "Pablum courses" designed to assure that all students graduate to hold down the dropout rate at the expense of bright and talented students desiring more difficult school work for college preparation.

• The Darwin theory of evolution as though it were scientific fact instead of mere conjecture with supportive evidence while refusing to allow the creation lesson in the Bible's book of Genesis to be taught in public schools.

The decline and fall and failure to reform public schools dates to the Supreme Court cases of 1962 and 1963 when prayer and Bible reading were abolished in probably the most controversial and perhaps even unconstitutional rulings ever made by the court. The fact that the issue is still prominent after more than 20 years and that faithful Christians have not given up the fight to restore God to the classrooms where His void has allowed Satan to move in, gives hope that the day will come when prayer and Bible reading will be restored and effective school reform can begin.

The Bible has more basic truths in it than all the textbooks now in use. Prayer for education at the outset of each day is more beneficial than all the secular curriculum now being taught without mention of God and His miracles which make the unfolding of science and other academic achievements possible.

In the last 20 years, since the ban on prayer and Bible reading, the American public has been fooled by the educators and academicians into mistakenly believing that the college students of the 1960's and 1970's were exceptionally gifted when in fact they were not. Many of these students became educators and academicians themselves and contributed to the ruination of public school curriculum. They lowered standards for social rather than academic reasons. The falsely believed that students who couldn't even spell correctly or speak coherently could nevertheless grasp moral, psychological and social theories beyond their capability. They failed to recognize that learning is best done in an orderly atmosphere instead of one where students "do their own thing" and turn into unruly mobs tinged with violence in the classroom and playground and parking lot. They spouted false doctrines in the face of traditional and proven facts. They have turned the schools upside down because they have turned their backs on God and His wisdom set out in the Bible. They believe in their own instruction instead of praying for God's guidance.

Until all these things are overcome by restoration of prayer and Bible reading in the public schools, there will be no substantial opportunity for true reform in American public education.

Education has been watered down and the old values once taught in the schools have been discarded in favor of "new ideas" that defy the precepts and the philosophy and history and policy of Western Civilization. A barbarian education philosophy has been introduced into the schools by sophisticated liberals who have convinced children entrusted into their care that the old American values of religion, patriotism, family and love are too old-fashioned and that the modern world requires a different set of standards and a different style of government.

Call it communism or call it "the new economic order" or call it the merging of the Third World into the rest of the world or call it whatever you like, but the point is that public school education in America today no longer cares about the fate of America and no longer cares about the religious or moral well-being of children. The radical turnabout in public school education was done in the name "peace and progress" but it fits perfectly nearly all the requirements of the Communist Manifesto.

The minds of millions of American children have been seduced over the past 40 years to think far differently than Americans of the past. This seduction has been fostered largely by the United States government after having made the decision to join the United Nations in 1945 and commit the resources of America—including human resources—to one-world internationalism.

Much of this can be traced directly to the U.N. and the influence it has brought to bear on member governments to change their education policies and systems to accommodate world citizenship.

THE U.N. CHANGED U.S. SCHOOLS

The man most responsible for implementing this new world policy through the U.S. was Dr. Brock Chisholm, a Canadian psychiatrist, who was selected by U.N. officials to establish the World Health Organization of the United Nations. That included mental health and in the reasoning of Chisholm and the U.N., mental health included education.

32

Dr. Chisholm headed the World Health Organization for five years, long enough to establish the new policy firmly in the U.N. and to inject the idea into the education systems—including teacher training—in member nations. Dr. Chisholm outlined the plan in speeches in Washington, D.C., and in New York in October, 1945, only two months after the end of World War II and the year the U.N. could finally function in what then passed for "peace."

Dr. Chisholm's speech was entitled "The Psychiatry of Enduring Peace and Social Progress." Here are some excerpts from the speech which became the master plan for world education after World War II:

"The only lowest common denominator of all civilizations and the only psychological force capable of producing these perversions is morality, the concept of right and wrong.

"We have swallowed all manner of poisonous certainties fed us by our parents, our Sunday and day school teachers, our politicians, our priests, our newspapers and others with a vested interest in controlling us . . . good and evil with which to keep children under control, with which to prevent free thinking, with which to impose local and familial and national loyalties . . . misguided by authoritarian dogma, bound by exclusive faith, stunted by inculcated loyalty.

"The freedom to observe and think freely has been destroyed or crippled by local certainties, by gods of local moralities, of local loyalty, gods that would keep each generation under the control of the old people, the elders, the shamans and the priests.

"Would it not be sensible to stop imposing our local prejudices and faiths on children? Freedom from moralities means freedom to observe, to think and behave sensibly, to the advantage of the person and the group, free from outmoded types of loyalties.

"That which stands in the way is ignorance and moral certainty, superstition and vested interest. There is something to be said for taking charge of our own destiny, if possible. If it cannot be done gently, it may have to be done roughly or even violently. That has happened before."

A close comparison of Dr. Chisholm's speech with the Communist Manifesto reveals he barely rewrote this document for his own speech, toning down some of the more radical rhetoric and claiming his theme was peace, progress and freedom.

In close association with the curriculum changes that began flowing into public schools after World War II came a relatively new education field called "counseling," which most people thought was some kind of job guidance advice. Many schools began hiring especially trained full-time counselors for their staffs and the counselors began regular interview and counseling sessions with nearly all the students in the school. It appeared harmless enough on the surface to the casual observer, the parent, the PTA, the education writers. But it was an entirely different and more sinister activity than it appeared to be.

Those knowledgeable about counseling knew that when school counseling is carried beyond 10 interviews it becomes the same as psychotherapy as used by psychiatrists in clinics. Its purpose is the reorganization of the personality. The American Psychiatric Association has said that psychotherapy may lead to dangerous mental conditions and has formally opposed the independent practice of psychotherapy even by licensed clinical psychologists. The ultimate results of psychotherapy are controversial but have not been proven beneficial.

The political motives of the originators and promoters of this program are found in a statement called "Mental Health and World Citizenship" by none other than—guess who—Dr. Brock Chisholm and others connected with the Josiah Macy Jr. Foundation.

Drawing upon Chisholm's work, the foundation and the American Council on Education co-published a book called *Emotion and the Educative Process* by Daniel A. Prescott whose thesis is that teachers should band together to use their position of influence to bring about changes in society and policies of government.

This psychiatric program as outlined in the works of Chisholm, Prescott and others became the pattern and guideline and precedent for school counseling-psychotherapy programs and psychological testing that were routinely adopted by the American education system with approval of the Department of Health, Education and Welfare.

Citing counseling and psychological testing results, educators began changing the traditional methods of teaching reading, writing, arithmetic, history, government, health education and every other subject in the schools. Along came "look-say" reading methods, the new math, the new science, sex education, group counseling, peer encounter sessions and all manner of new educational techniques that left parents befuddled about what is going on in the schools.

34

ARE THEY SCHOOLS OR
PSYCHIATRIC INSTITUTIONS?

American public schools are becoming less schools for learning basic education skills and more like some kind of psychiatric clinic.

Many American public schools routinely subject students to psychological examinations as part of entrance requirements or periodic evaluation. School counseling in connection with these examinations has in some places posed questions to students concerning their sexual behavior and attitudes as a general part of sex education in the schools. Students have been asked to supply information concerning the behavior and attitudes of family members as part of a sociological profile or dossier compiled on individual students. There are laws against this kind of arrogance by school officials but the laws are not enforced and are shot through with loopholes.

The New York City Board of Education recently published a new Sex Education Program book as a guideline for teaching sex education in the schools there. It suggests teachers involve students in what educators love to call "role playing," that is, making up hypothetical situations involving the students and let them act out the solution.

New York's guidelines suggests the following: pretend your parents are getting a divorce; pretend you are having a conflict with your parents; pretend someone you know is pregnant and discuss her options, ranging from teen-age marriage to abortion, single parenthood, adoption or foster care; pretend your boyfriend or girlfriend has told you he or she has a venereal disease. Pupils from kindergarten to grade 2 are asked to tell the class what happens in their home when mother is expecting a baby and to discuss some of the ways their parents show love for one another. Children are encouraged to interview grandparents or older family adults and ask personal questions about their behavior when they were younger.

Recently, during the nuclear war freeze craze touched off by the Soviet Union propaganda machine in 1979 as it tried to persuade American opinion to stop the deployment of missiles to match the Soviet missiles in Europe, the National Education Association — the liberal teachers' union — instituted a course available to public schools and adopted by some to instill in students fear, guilt and despair about nuclear weapons. That's not education, it's psychiatric treatment!

These two subjects—sex and anti-nuclear war — are the only two subjects in the entire NEA curriculum guides that are

35

available to a student from kindergarten through high school graduation every year . . . not English, not math, not science, not history — but sex and nuclear war courses, which incidentally invade the personal privacy of students by prying into family political affiliations and attitudes, and by psychologically trying to persuade students to conform with the politics and prejudices set out in the curriculum guides.

One student, writing a term paper as a climax to a nuclear war course, wrote: "These days I just try not to think about my future, because I have a hard time seeing one. I want to do something with my life, but who cares about me? Besides, we're all going to be blown up anyway."

Is prayer and Bible reading in the schools worse than that? Would it be worse for that student to find out that God loves him, created him, gives him life and has a plan for his life, than it is to teach him to write "who cares. . .we're all going to get blown up anyway?"

Prayer and Bible reading are needed in our public schools today more than ever to offset these bizarre sexual and political teachings. Instead of being psychologically abused by sex and war courses, children need to be taught about the positive things about this country, the positive things about basic education skills that can equip them with hope and care and faith in their own future and the future of the country.

Some of the stuff the schools are teaching now couldn't suit the communists more than if it had been drawn up in the Kremlin propaganda office for distribution to American school children.

There is no reason why Christians should have to establish separate school systems for their children. Christians have as much right to the public schools as anyone else. The establishment of a separate system of Christian schools is a step backward to the days when there was a separate system of schools for black children. Christians have a right to the public schools and right to say what is to be taught in them.

Americans were sadly mistaken when they let the federal government persuade them to accept federal aid for local schools. The government lied when it said there would be no strings attached and the local schools would remain under local control.

The trouble with the public schools in America is that they didn't go from local to federal control, they went from local to international control with a federal government acting as the internationalists' agent. The federal government had already committed itself to internationalism with membership in the

United Nations and all that entailed, including an education system of world citizenship rather than national citizenship.

COURTS "SOWED" A WHIRLWIND

The United States Supreme Court has become a government tyranny because of its rulings barring prayer and Bible reading from public schools, making the murder of unborn babies by abortion on demand legal, and allowing the teaching of homosexuality.

By banishing morality and endorsing violence, the Supreme Court sowed the winds of change 20 years ago and America is reaping the whirlwind of moral abuse and violence among America's younger generation today.

The Supreme Court made a basic error in judgment on those landmark decisions. Its error was the mistaken opinion that prayer and Bible reading in the schools violated separation of church and state mentioned indirectly in the First Amendment.

President Reagan believes the Supreme Court was in error and said so in a speech in Washington. He said: "When I hear the First Amendment used today as a reason to keep traditional moral values away from policymaking, I am shocked. The First Amendment was not written to protect the people and their laws from religious values; it was written to protect those values from Government tyranny."

Amen, Mr. President, and that's why I charge today that the U.S. Supreme Court has become a government tyranny.

As for the whirlwind being reaped today, I submit the following:

ITEM: So many students are going to school armed in the Houston, Texas schools that the school district purchased both hand-held and walk-through weapons detectors in an effort to disarm youngsters before they enter the classroom. A 19-year-old high school senior was shot and killed in a Houston school counselor's office by her 21-year-old estranged husband, also a student, who then shot himself once in the head but survived.

ITEM: In Los Angeles, the nation's largest school district, police estimate that 60 per cent of the students use drugs two or three times a week and up to 25 per cent are "stoned most of the time," according to Deputy Police Chief Lew Ritter.

ITEM: Dr. James Strain, president of the American Academy of Pediatrics, said in Chicago that teen-age suicide, alcoholism and drug abuse have "grown to such epidemic proportions that living to adulthood may be an unrealistic expectation for many youths."

ITEM: In Tulsa, Oklahoma, the home of this ministry and of Oral Roberts and of many other religious headquarters, a 14-year-old girl was abducted by several young men who disrobed her, forced her to pose for pornographic photos, tortured her and raped her. Police Sgt. Don Spillers said police are coming across more and more frequent cases of this kind with adolescent pornography as the motive.

ITEM: The Nebraska Prevention Center for Alcohol and Drug Abuse reported recently that a survey of 4,500 students in grades 7 through 12 showed almost 70 per cent had used alcohol in the previous month and that some 40 per cent had been drunk in the two previous weeks.

ITEM: The New York Times ran a story about youth gangs, muggings, robberies, rapes, assaults and even murders under this headline—"Efforts to Fight Youth Crime Called Ineffective in New York."

ITEM: In Beaufort, N.C., two boys held a principal and teacher as hostages before being disarmed of their loaded shotgun.

ITEM: A national survey by a major news magazine has revealed that among high school seniors, 72 per cent use alcohol today compared to 68 per cent in 1975; 34 per cent use marijuana compared with 27 per cent in 1975; 12 per cent use some form of prescription stimulants compared with 9 per cent eight years ago and 5 per cent use cocaine compared with 2 per cent then.

ITEM: The Center for Communicative Disease Control, which keeps abortion statistics on a national basis since the slaying became "legal" in 1973, reports that about 15 million unborn babies have been killed by abortions authorized by the Supreme Court during the past 10 years, about 1.5 million a year.

I could go on and on but to what avail? The story is that the youth of America are much worse off today than they were 20 years ago. Their school work shows it. Collectively, test scores, reading ability, mathematical understanding, speech and writing skills, and other basic educational requirements have all deteriorated sadly since the early 1960s when the Supreme Court refused moral guidance to school children.

At the same time, in the 1960s, sex education became popular and fashionable in the schools and since then the number of unwanted teenage pregnancies have skyrocketed along with the rate of venereal diseases among young people and reports of sexual promiscuity, aberrant sexual behavior and downright sadism and torture involving teens. Teenage

38

runaways number in the millions. Teenage suicide increases.

Only a few are ever salvaged from depths of these various sins when they are discovered and treatment afforded. The untold and unmeasured heartbreak in millions and millions of American families is the price paid for these Supreme Court and education system innovations, to say nothing of the pain suffered by the individual youngster.

We must quit quibbling over the debatable interpretations of the Supreme Court about whether school prayer and Bible reading involved separation of church and state—the fate of these young Americans, the fate of the future of the nation now hanging in the balance, is far more important than these legal hair-splittings promoted largely by professional Johnny-come-lately liberals who stand to profit by promotion of these unconventional standards in courts and schools.

We must ask ourselves if our children's and our grandchildren's and our nation's future is more important than theoretical arguments about separation of church and state. We must consider whether President Reagan is right when he says the Constitution was not meant to protect the people and their laws from religious values but to protect those values from government tyranny.

We must decide whether we are going to do nothing about this problem, whether we are going to continue to rely on schools without moral guidance, whether we want to overrule the Supreme Court with new and stronger laws and Constitutional amendments designed to remedy these national ailments.

Children can easily be taught right from wrong unless those responsible for the teaching are not allowed to do it. These are God's children and His spirit is in each of them. They have consciences, that voice of God inside them that provides them a standard upon which to base their behavior and separate themselves from animals, a soul as it were. Proper moral guidance and training, the reminder of that spiritual self that can be provided by prayer and Bible reading, the love of country that can be inspired by the flag and patriotic songs, all these can be and must be restored to our schools if we are to save the youth and the future of America.

THE NEA AND COMMUNISM

"Communism continues to infiltrate the schools and curriculum of American education."

I have been saying this for years and the National Education and the Civil Liberties Union and all the other liberals have attacked me for it and said that I didn't know what I was talking about.

Well here is some **more proof.** The National Education Association has joined the current misnamed "peace movement" designed to weaken the defense of the United States while ignoring the Soviet military buildup. The NEA is installing in the schools a new curriculum about "conflict and nuclear war" that is filled with the kind of propaganda that could turn millions of American school children into peaceniks and appeasers if not outright communist sympathizers.

Part of this plan is included in a classroom resource guide called **Creating Our Future,** published by a liberal-leftist outfit headed by Roberta Snow and called "Educators for Social Responsibility" or ESR. Their plan is to end the arms race, starting with propaganda aimed at getting America to disarm first. The literature says this: "Through this organization we can bring peace education into the classroom and become a powerful political force. We can make a difference."

They sure can! They can make a difference in favor of communism! The guide this leftist outfit published for the schools—and it is being embraced and adopted by the National Education Association—is full of lies and communist propaganda. For example, it describes the communist-controlled U.S. Peace Council as a "multi-national, multi-racial, organization that merges the struggle for peace, detente and national liberation with the movements of labor and community for a better life."

That's a lie. The U.S. Peace Council is the American office of the World Peace Council which alledgedly was founded and is still financed by the Kremlin and headed by a communist from India. To these phony councils, national liberation is translated as revolution; peace as appeasement; and detente as a one-way street favoring communism.

It takes only a minimum amount of research to trace the communist-origin of the World and U.S. Peace Councils. American educators who are swallowing this classroom guide called **Creating Our Future** without knowing that or finding it out are either ignorant about communism or in collusion with communism.

This communist guide tells another lie. It says that in 1983, 61 per cent of every federal income dollar went to military-related spending. That's not true. The fact is that only about 26 per cent of every federal dollar has a relation to military spending.

Other evidence of communism in American education is seen

in this lastest campus mania to shout down and deprive freedom of speech for any pro-American or U.S. government speaker on college campuses. That's what happened to America's former UN Representative, Jeanne Kirkpatrick, at the University of California. But every liberal, leftist, communist or cult speaker is given a respectable hearing.

Here's more: Dimitri K. Simes, a senior associate at the Carnegie Endowment for International Peace, has been named Research Professor of Soviet Studies at the Johns Hopkins School of Advanced International Studies. This action is part of the leftist-liberal syndrome so prevalent on most American college campuses. So-called "Soviet studies" are growing in popularity while hardly any American free-enterprise free republic studies can be found anywhere in U.S. education.

The new disarmament and appeasement curriculum in American education will weaken the will to resist communism and will plant the seeds in the minds of America's future leaders that it is America that is wrong in this world struggle between freedom and totalitarian tyranny.

There had been some hope that American education might emerge from the Dark Ages and give kids a chance to get ahead in life but the schools have resisted reform.

The hopes of millions of American parents and school-supporting taxpayers were lifted in the spring of 1983 when President Reagan's National Commission on Education Excellence reported the sorry state of the schools and outlined a program of reform.

Today the schools are still sorry and the reform plan has been killed by the teachers' union known as the National Education Association which stubbornly contends that only money is needed to improve education, despite more than two decades of evidence to the contrary.

The NEA is not to be underestimated. It has strong friends in Congress. It was the NEA urging that prompted many Congressmen to vote against legislation that would have paved the way for restoration of prayer and Bible reading in public schools, still the number one need of American education today.

Without God's blessing, public education is doomed. The NEA and other entrenched education interests fight prayer and Bible reading every step of the way and argue that God, morality, spirituality and religion in general must have no place in education. American schools have gone downhill since the Supreme Court rulings of the early 1960's which effectively banned prayer and Bible reading in the classroom.

41

The NEA, while resisting prayer and Bible reading, embraced communist propaganda concerning America's national defense by introducing into the curriculum of all schools which would accept it, the misnamed "peace program" that might as well have been written in the Kremlin for all the good it had to say about our national defense and security policy.

The liberals who control the NEA tried to scare the wits out of millions of American school kids with the phony "peace" program that played upon the horror of nuclear war, criticized American defense expenditures on missiles and other military hardware and promoted a Utopian dream of effortless peace without military strength to support it. This unrealistic teaching was introduced into many American classrooms during the height of the communist-sponsored "peace" campaign designed to halt the placement of American missiles in Europe to offset the Soviet's already-placed SS 20s intimidating Western Europe.

Despite the NEA's acceptance of Soviet policy and resistance to school prayer and Bible reading, some states have moved to reform their schools anyway, only to run into local and state NEA opposition.

In Texas, for example, Governor Mark White appointed a Select Committee on Public Education headed by multimillionaire H. Ross Perot, a man whose past record of patriotism frightens the communist-appeasers within the NEA.

Perot's committee came up with a plan to overhaul Texas public schools, establish merit pay and promotion for teachers, institute a curriculum that was something other than anti-American, demand student behavior short of riot and anarchy, and insisted upon other improvements the NEA has opposed traditionally.

The Texas State Teachers Association met not long ago and spent most of its convention time shooting spitwads at Perot and his plan. What the teachers said was needed in Texas is a 24 per cent pay raise for teachers across the board, or a flat $4,100 a year raise, whichever is greater. The Texas teachers came out against such reforms as competency testing of teachers, a longer school year, a longer school day, less emphasis on vocational training and more on basic academics such as reading, writing and arithmetic and stricter discipline.

Perot's recommendation for Texas was to reduce expenditures for vocational education, which receives 25 per cent of every dollar compared with 40 per cent for the basics. The state's vo-tech authorities say that is unacceptable. And the state school board's organization was against Perot's plan to make school boards appointive instead of elected.

So there was trouble in Texas and many other states are experiencing the same thing in their efforts to reform education against the wishes of the NEA union and moss-backed educational hierarchy who helped get the schools into the mess they are, in the first place.

The trouble with public schools is that they have a law-given monopoly and are not responsive to what in economics is called "the marketplace." The marketplace puts its fossils out of business but not so the public sector where monopoly is the way of life.

The NEA-school monopoly position basically boils down to this: Nothing Can Be Done, jobs and tenure and seniority cannot be changed or challenged, new ideas from outside the school system are unacceptable, old ideas within the school system cannot be thought through again, the public should shut up and pay up.

Unfortunately, the ones who suffer in the dinosaur society of public education in America are the children. For them, education has been homogenized, reduced to its lowest common denominator, robbed of moral guidance and spiritual inspiration, removed from the presence of God and isolated from new ideas.

Except in rare cases of rich school districts and exceptional teacher-administration enlightenment, look for the schools to sink deeper into the Dark Ages which enveloped them some 20 years ago.

The Presidential Reform Commission made the not-so-surprising discovery that there is a connection between the educational system and the nation's economic success. Is it any wonder we have had recessions, work stoppages, strikes, unemployment, inflation, boom-and-bust economy when millions of so-called "graduates" of American schools are functionally illiterate? They can't read, write, figure out simple math, balance their checkbooks, make correct change, follow simple instructions or perform any business procedure more complicated than making a telephone call.

But they know about sex! They know how to drive! They know how to sit around and have bull sessions! They know how to take coffee and cigarette breaks! They have an interest in sports and have spent hours upon hours in front of the TV set and also at physical education ... which as Timothy says in the Bible: *"Bodily excercise profiteth little."* But our schools spend millions upon millions on gymnasiums and football stadiums and **nothing on Bibles!**

43

The schools in America must be completely overhauled and reformed if we are to continue as a nation, if we are to have a future . . . and the place to begin is with restoration of prayer and Bible reading . . . and all the rest will come along once we get our schools right with God again.

The removal of prayer and Bible reading from the public schools was a logical step in the entire process of replacing the old traditional American education system with the new United Nations world citizenship curriculum.

The result has, of course, been a disaster for American public education as the National Commission on Excellence in Education report reveals. But it has not been a disaster for America's enemies and rivals.

And the best the federal government can do—and it's done far too much already—is recommend the same old thing: spend more money on the schools.

If there is to be a future for America, American patriots, including American Christians, must regain control of the public schools. The best the government has been able to recommend is to do patchwork on an already destroyed school system. What is needed is a complete rebuilding job.

' The rebuilding of education in America must be as thorough as was its recent destruction if America is to survive. And it must start with a 180 degree change of course in the policy, the philosophy, of education. The United Nations plan must be thrown out and the American plan put back in its place. The godless must be ejected from the schools and God restored and honored with prayer and with Bible reading. There is nothing wrong with studying such theories as evolution so long as they are studied in the perspective that it is just that, a theory and one without evidence to prove it. Creation as presented in the Bible should be taught right along with evolution.

Education is the key to America's future and prayer and Bible reading is the key to quality education. It is urgent that America get on with the job of restoring prayer and Bible reading to the public schools, of cleansing the curriculum of immoral teachings and of reforming the structure of education so that our children and grandchildren and great-grandchildren will live in freedom, true peace, joy and righteousness instead of being degraded into what will eventually become communist slavery if nothing is done to change the schools.

Chapter 3

FAILURE OF THE AMERICAN SPIRIT

Just as America has turned its back on God's advice in the Bible for achieving prosperity by embracing covetousness and greed in its financial affairs instead of sharing with God; just as it has turned its back on God's Word, the Holy Bible, in the schools without prayer, so has America turned its back on God in many other ways spiritually.

We don't have to look far to find America's spiritual failure. The moral crisis of our time is the murder of 1.5 million innocent unborn babies a year by abortion. The "legalization" of abortion by the U.S. Supreme Court in 1973 is one of the darkest chapters in the high court's dark history of recent times. God may forgive us many things but the shedding of the innocent blood of His babies could try His mercy and patience and grace beyond the breaking point. If America does not return to the days of banning abortion the same as banning murder, it stands at risk in God's eyes.

Sin runs rampant in America today. Crime, rape, pornography, homosexuality and lesbianism, divorce, adultery, fornication, sexual promiscuity, drug abuse, profanity, violence, disrespect for authority and for elders, blasphemy, drunkenness, covetousness, prostitution, idolatry (of both self and money), worshipping strange and lewd "gods," general wickedness and all manner of other sin corrupts America and its religious spirit.

In one of several books about the sin and crime of abortion, a book called *Thou Shall Not Kill . . . His Babies*, published by Americans For Life, the pro-life arm of Christian Crusade, I said that, "Abortion is the major moral crisis of our time," and that quote was picked up and repeated by wire services and published in much of the national media. I still believe that and believe that abortion is the one national sin that God just may not forgive America unless we reverse that ungodly 1973 Supreme Court ruling with a Constitutional Amendment banning abortion or whatever it takes to change it.

Let's Abort Abortion

Since the U.S. Supreme Court legalized abortion during the "FULL TERM" of a woman's pregnancy on January 22, 1973, our nation has witnessed the wholesale slaughter of unborn children and it goes on night and day in every single state including your own.

In fact, more babies are killed by abortion every year in the U.S.A. than the combined populations of three of America's major cities . . . Miami, Florida, Kansas City, Missouri and Minneapolis, Minnesota.

In spite of the fact that many people are shocked and upset when I use words like "murder" or "killing" to describe abortion, that's exactly what it is! We will only be able to stop abortion in the United States when Americans come to understand exactly what abortion is. ABORTION IS LEGALIZED KILLING! It's the murder of a tiny human being who is defenseless against the abortionist's deadly and inhuman surgical instruments.

DON'T LET THE PRO-ABORTIONISTS AND/OR CHILD KILLERS CONVINCE YOU THAT LIFE EXISTS ONLY AFTER THE CHILD IS BORN. That is contrary to fact. If the baby killers can just get the American people to think that an aborted baby is nothing more than medical waste, then they have won their battle.

When I ask you to support Christian Crusade's "AMERICANS FOR LIFE" to save the lives of unborn, unwanted little humans, I want you to remember that a baby . . . the so-called FETUS in that mother's womb . . . breathes, sleeps, and wakes up when he hears noises from the outside world. He hiccups, swallows and sucks his thumb just like a newborn baby. Furthermore, he feels pain. He tastes. He can be taught things and has measurable brainwaves. If that isn't life, I don't know what it is.

ABORTION CLINICS are allegedly selling the little dead babies to cosmetic manufacturers for their use in the preparation of shampoos, facial and hand creams and even soap. I feel from the depth of my heart that our raising this issue of the use of human COLLAGEN in the cosmetic industry will deal a DEATH BLOW to the abortionists and their satanic cause.

Therefore, we declare for the whole world to hear, that, as Christians, we are anti-abortionists and against euthanasia . . . that is, the killing of the unwanted elderly. We have respect for human life; therefore, we support AMERICANS FOR LIFE in its unending battle to get abortion and euthanasia declared UNCONSTITUTIONAL!

Planned Death

Planned Parenthood of Chicago went into murder by abortion in such a big way in 1984 that it withdrew from the United Way charity so it wouldn't hurt fund raising for the community drive.

The withdrawal announcement apparently was intended by Planned Parenthood officials to make the organization look charitable and big-hearted itself. But how big-hearted can an organization be that is planning to go into the wholesale murder business?

Planned Parenthood's sex education programs and contraception counseling was already hurting the United Way in Chicago, where Catholic contributors had begun withholding funds from United Way only because of Planned Parenthood's activities. In 1983, Cardinal Joseph Bernardin, Catholic archbishop of Chicago, had suggested that Catholics either give to Catholic charities only or specifically designate their gifts to a United Way agency. The implication was that the church was boycotting United Way because of Planned Parenthood.

Planned Parenthood had been receiving about $150,000 annually from United Way. Even in withdrawing, United Way gave Planned Parenthood a "one-time" transition gift of $250,000, which to the more cynical looks suspiciously like a payoff to Planned Parenthood to get out.

Planned Parenthood is now opening its own death chambers, adding abortion to its sex education and contraceptive planning activities. There are already some 5,500 abortion clinics blighting the American scene and the baby murder business is so profitable it has now attracted Planned Parenthood as competition.

Some innocent unborn child is being murdered by abortion in America every 21 seconds, a total of 4,000 a day, about 1.5 million a year, or some 15 million plus since the U.S. Supreme Court ruled in favor of abortion in 1973.

If in any other area of humanity, 4,000 persons a day were being deliberately murdered, exterminated, the cry of outrage from the news media and the pulpit and the politicians would be heard to the heavens. But because in these cases it is "only abortion," "only business as usual," an apathetic America goes its ungodly way harming God's little children, disregarding His warning, *"Thou shalt not kill."* And He might have added "... My babies."

United Way of Chicago spokesman David Dalton was quoted as saying, "There has been a tradition that United Way does not fund abortions." That sounded very weak in light of the $250,000 "transition" gift to Planned Parenthood as it plans to go full-tilt into the abortion business, despite understandings that none of the United Way funds would be used to pay for abortions.

That line of reasoning is similar to that of the National and World Councils of Churches which sends money to communist guerrillas throughout the world, ostensibly for medical supplies, not military supplies.

The point is that Planned Parenthood will be able to "free up" some other $250,000 now from other sources to spend on abortion clinics that it might have had to use elsewhere if United Way of Chicago had not made the quarter-million dollar payoff. It has been proven that in Zimbabwe and Southeast Asia and elsewhere that communists were able to use short and hard-pressed general funds for purchasing armaments instead of medical supplies once the Councils of Churches medical funds were in hand. Such understandings are nothing more than double bookkeeping and neither Planned Parenthood nor United Way of Chicago should do much self-congratulating over the abortion deal.

Abortion Horrors

A Dallas, Texas, abortion clinic nurse who converted to Christianity after witnessing scenes of horror for months in the murder chamber where she worked, told her story to a Texas religious publication. Following are the highlights, or perhaps they should be called the lowlights, of that interview:

• Most of the abortions were not legal, even under the U.S. Supreme Court abortion ruling, because they were done to women who were from 16 to 22 weeks pregnant.

• The doctor operating the clinic could make more money from one 10-minute abortion than he could from supervising a nine-month pregnancy and then delivering the baby. On some full-term pregnancies and deliveries, he made $625, which he could easily equal with six abortions in a day.

• Although the doctor was an obstetrician, he performed

abortions before and after office hours, and during lunch hours when the office was closed to obstetric patients because too many of the abortion patients were what he called "screamers" who upset his regular obstetric patients.

• One-half to two-thirds of the doctor's practice eventually became devoted to abortions. The cost to a patient was $110 for pregnancies up to 12 weeks because that is what Medicaid would pay for an abortion. Many younger girls simply used abortion as a lazy form of birth control as long as Medicaid paid all the costs. One 17-year-old girl had three abortions in one year, all paid for by Medicaid.

• A suction device was used for abortions up until 12 to 14 weeks. After that, an instrument like spaghetti tongs was inserted into the cervix and parts of the unborn baby were simply grabbed by the pincers and pulled off, causing the baby to bleed to death.

• After one especially horrifying abortion with much blood and screaming and vomiting, the nurse asked the doctor, "My God, are we going to hell?" He replied, "Well, honey, if we are, I'll be there first waiting on you."

• After the nurse quit the job and accepted Christ, she said that abortion is the killing of a human being, there is no other word for it but murder.

In Defense of the Unborn

The Pro-Life movement is the most ecumenical movement in America today. It is also the most divisive! It is ecumenical because it unites the various Christian churches throughout the country. It is devisive because it draws a line between those who believe in God and want to obey His laws and those who ignore God and don't want to be bound by the moral laws He has made.

When the U.S. Supreme Court declared, that "the ancient religion" did not ban abortion, the Court clearly meant paganism, since both Judaism and Christianity did ban abortion.

The Court also rejected the "apparent rigidity" of the time-honored Hippocratic Oath, to which doctors have subscribed for more than 2,000 years. The famous oath pledged not to give a pregnant woman anything that would cause abortion.

Going way beyond its field, the Court dabbled in theology, philosophy and even medicine by declaring that "new embyological data" indicates that conception is "a process over time, rather than an event."

The Court was simply seeking an excuse to justify taking

the life of unborn babies. Conception is "a process" of, at the very most, a few days duration, and this certainly does not justify taking the life of a baby several months later. Yet the Court legalized abortion right through the nine months of pregnancy.

First the Court banned any mention of God in public schools through prayer or even Bible readings, then it rejected the almost universal consensus of Christian moral teachers all down the centuries on abortion.

We can hardly expect God to bless our country as long as 1½ million unborn babies are killed every year in America in defiance of the Commandment.

Every argument in favor of abortion can be used equally well for taking the life of a baby after it has been born. Birth is merely a change of residence. The outdated notion that an unborn baby does not deserve protection until he or she is "viable" is just another excuse, not a reason, for taking unborn life. In relying on the shallow argument of viability, the Court is on a collision course with itself, as Justice Sandra O'Connor has observed, since the age for viability changes every year with progress in medical science. Thank God we have Ronald Reagan, a firm Pro-Life advocate in the White House.

He has said that he will not appoint anyone to the Court who is for abortion. He has already appointed one Pro-Life advocate in the person of Justice O'Connor. This has changed the complexion of the Court from the notorious 7-2 for abortion to 6-3.

At this writing, the six Justices who are pro-abortion, five are aged 73-77. They are not only walking on thin ice because of their age, several of them are also in poor health. With the appointment of just one more Justice to the court, the vote will have changed from 6-3 to 5-4 in favor of abortion.

Then with the appointment of just one more Pro-Life Justice, the Court will be solidly in favor of the unborn child, 5-4. President Reagan has not only the opportunity of appointing two more judges to the Court, he will probably have the chance to appoint three. That will make the Court 6-3 in favor of the unborn child, instead of the present 6-3 against the defense of the unborn.

We cannot let abortion continue to kill 4,000 daily without letting euthanasia, the so-called "mercy-killing" of the aged or retarded, and other forms of human slaughter take over in our society.

As long as unborn babies can be sacrificed on the altar of

convenience, none of us is safe. Nor will our country continue to have the blessing of God!

Killing Handicapped Infants is the "New Fashion"

Killing new-born babies believed to have mental or physical birth defects is the new "fashion" among American intellectual elitists and is a natural follow-up to the U.S. abortion policy that has resulted in the murder of 15 million unborn children in the past 10 years.

These "elitists" include certain medical doctors, supposedly intelligent parents who want nothing but perfect children, judges who have made fatal rulings regarding newly-born babies, all supported by a host of news media writers and commentators along with other advocates of infanticide whose lives and careers are not endangered while they play God, deciding who is to live and who is not.

In Greek and Roman days, infants with physical defects were frequently killed in the mistaken belief that physically normal children would eventually breed a perfect super-race. Hitler made the same mistake. Now an American elite class is doing the same thing but adding infants whom they believe might be mentally defective to those with physical defects.

The new wave of infant killing came into vogue in 1982 when Indiana Superior Court Judge John G. Baker ruled in the so-called Baby Doe Case of Bloomington, Indiana, that parents had the right to order their baby—born with Downs Syndrome and a malformed esophagus — to order the child *starved to death!* The ruling was against an ignored federal law, Section 504 of the Rehabilitation Act of 1973, which says it is unlawful for hospitals receiving federal funds (and that includes most of them these days) to withhold "nutritional sustenance or medical or surgical treatment to correct a life-threatening condition" if such withholding is based on the fact that the patient (adults are covered, too) is handicapped.

The Baby Doe case of 1982 was followed by the Baby Jane Doe case of 1983 in New York in which Dr. George Newman advised the parents of a little girl needing two operations to close an open spinal column and to drain excess fluid surrounding the brain to withhold treatment and allow the baby to die. The parents followed the doctor's recommendation and refused permission for the operations.

Then there is the case of the non-fiction book entitled *The Long Dying of Baby Andrew,* the story of baby Andrew Stinson, born 16 weeks prematurely with several physical disorders who died six months after intensive care treatment.

51

The book, written by the parents, is more about their own self-pity than concern for the baby. The mother would not touch or even visit her infant son, because, as she wrote:

"I can't face the nurses, this month's doctor-stranger — the people who know all out our marriage and our finances and understand nothing about me."

The parents first wanted an abortion but gestation was too far along. They were assured by doctors that the baby would die shortly after birth, instead he lived six months. The parents said they were driven to psychiatric care and a marriage counselor by the experience.

The liberal, leftist news media has taken up the defense of American infanticide if a child is not born perfect enough to suit parents and doctors. In the case of Baby Jane Doe, two operations would have saved the baby's life but the media argued that such operations would only be "life prolonging" or in effect, a pointless exercise in medical expertise. The catch phrase "life prolonging" was used by the *New York Post, the New York Daily News, USA Today, Lesley Stahl on CBS, Tom Brokaw on NBC, Peter Jennings on ABC and Ted Koppel on ABC's Nightline.* The pity is no one knew for certain how long life would be prolonged. Most thought about 20 years because a doctor in the case merely testified that "20 years is possible" in response to a leading question that had asked if 20 years was possible. What about 60 years? No one asked that. So the media jumped on 30 years as a guess and ran with it in support of the killing of Baby Jane Doe.

When President Reagan ordered the U.S. Department of Health and Human Services to notify hospitals of section 504 of the 1973 Rehabilitation Act, the Reagan-haters in the news media criticized him for being "intrusive" into private family affairs, ignoring the fact that he is sworn to uphold federal laws. The media blew it up into an alleged conflict between state and private control of personal lives.

While the media attacked Reagan and championed the killing of the Baby Does, they remained silent on the issue and the moral question of baby killing or infanticide. This is the same mind-set that approves abortion as a personal matter between a woman and her physician without regard to the unborn child to be killed. Now that type of thinking has moved into the area of live babies, new-born infants with various kinds of birth defects, supporting the right to kill them without regarding their right to live. This is what we mean by "elitists" in America playing God.

Modern medical technology is now able to save the lives of

52

not only defective babies in a mother's womb but also of infants born with what formerly were believed to be fatal birth defects, such as spina bifida (open spinal column) and hydrocephalus (excessive fluid around the brain) and many others.

The abortionists and elitists now cannot be certain when a fetus is "viable" and modern medical technology and expertise for correcting many birth defects negates their argument for "mercy killing." Mercy for who, the baby or the parents?

In the case of Baby Doe, who had Down's Syndrome, the media latched onto the catch phrase "severely retarded" and used it repeatedly, as they had done with "life prolonging" in the Baby Jane Doe case. What they did not report was that there is a long waiting list of couples willing to adopt Down's Syndrome children; that the IQs of Down's Syndrome people are generally between 25 and 60 with some classified with normal intelligence; that there is no way to determine at birth how retarded a child might be, much less to say as early as birth that it will be "severely retarded." The media, either ignorantly or purposefully, plays into the hands of the elitist baby killers, joining their ranks to mold public opinion in favor of infanticide.

All these elitists in medicine, the news media, and the political and social scientists fail to report with words and photographs the agonizing deaths, cries and suffering of babies dying from inflicted starvation and withholding of medical treatment by physicians supposedly sworn to save lives instead of deliberately taking them.

This is the fall-out and legacy of abortion. Once death can be legally decreed, where does it stop? Many of the infant deaths have been caused by the God-players simply ignoring such laws as Section 504. To them, there apparently is no difference in killing a baby in the womb or killing a baby shortly out of the womb. Killing leads to more killing.

Governor Lamm of Colorado advocates killing off the unproductive elderly to provide more opportunity for young people and relieving them of tax burdens to support the elderly. This philosophy of state euthanasia is another legacy of abortion. Who's next? The handicapped, perhaps, or the inmates of mental hospitals? How about criminals, no matter the type of crime, misdemeanor or felony? After all, as abortion-infanticide-euthanasia thinking goes, what difference does it make if they are going to be any burden whatsoever on society? Doesn't anyone understand *me*, as the mother of Baby Andrew put it, emphasizing her role in the *"me generation.* " Never mind Baby Andrew, what about *me?*

Abortion was only the first step. Infanticide has now become fashionable and acceptable among the God-playing elite, supported by the liberal, leftist national news media. Euthanasia is next, and the elite God-players and their media friends will be the ones to decide to whom euthanasia shall be applied and how far the killing will become fashionable and acceptable from there.

God help America! How far we have come from our Christian founding. We have arrived at the point where man, scientific man, the Age of Reason man, now considers himself above God.

Instead of moving back toward God, America seems to be moving farther away from Him. When is America going to put God back into the schools, back into the hospitals, back into the courts, back into the universities, even back into some of the churches that seem to have forgotten what the Bible says about Him? Will the news media ever accept God?

All fails without Christ. Jesus Christ is still the hope of the world and the hope of America. The world and America need Christ now more than ever before. It is Satan's doing, this murder of babies, this godless philosophy of an elite deciding arbitrarily who shall live and who shall die without due process of law, or by judges who simply ignore law.

The power of Satan now gripping the schools and rapidly infiltrating the fields of medicine and law cannot be stemmed by man. Only God can defeat Satan and He shall, through His Son, Jesus Christ. Americans should be praying that that day comes as soon as possible — or be prepared to pay with the lives of millions of more babies murdered by abortion and infanticide.

Drugs Defeating America

Communism is doing everything in its power to ship drugs into America to destroy the moral fabric of this country.

Southeast Asia is being turned into a huge poppy farm for the refinement of heroin to be shipped to America. Colombia, in South America, is trans-shipping hundreds of thousands of pounds of cocaine annually through Cuba and sometimes directly into the United States.

This drug traffic aimed at destroying America is of Satan. . and communism is of Satan. The two evil forces combined, drugs and communism, are proving lethal to America and world freedom. The civilized world hangs in the balance at this moment as drugs poison America from within and communism is isolating us and surrounding us.

God help us! I want you to pray for your deliverance as you read this report I regretfully must make:

The drug capital of the United States, in usage and sales and traffic, is New York City. A recent flood of cocaine has swept over New York, dropping the street price and making drugs available to school children for the price of a lunch.

New York dealers selling to school children laughingly call them "little garbage heads."

The Substances Abuse Services Division of the state of New York reports that the number of state residents using cocaine has doubled — **Doubled!** — since 1981. It says nearly 500,000 state residents, most of them in New York City, now use cocaine at least — **at least!** once a week. A record number of patients have applied for state-financed drug treatment.

As many women as men are using cocaine. Dr. Arnold Washburn, a drug researcher and psychologist in New York says that women are being introduced to cocaine through romantic courtships. Instead of candy or flowers, men now routinely bring women cocaine as a gift, Dr. Washburn said.

New York hospitals are reporting an alarming increase in the number of young people suffering seizures, strokes and premature heart attacks as a result of drug use.

Police say heroin addicts are more inclined to commit violent crimes, such as robbery to support their expensive habit, and rape as an outlet for drug-driven aggressiveness. Cocaine addicts commit more than 200 crimes each during a year. **200 crimes each!** In a year! A crime every other day! Most of the cocaine crimes are petty thefts, burglaries, embezzlements and forgeries.

The New York City jails report that in three years, the number of inmates who underwent drug detoxification rose from 7,679 to 13,046, nearly doubling the inmates.

Officials say cocaine and heroin use is at an all-time high and still spiraling. The junkies on the street are being interviewed and quoted in the *New York Times,* saying the drug scene is great . . . that there has never been so much of it so cheap as there is now. One junkie, a "big garbage head," said this: "Even if they clean up Avenue D (a notorious Lower East Side street sales drug market) there is always somewhere else to get it—East Harlem, College Avenue in the Bronx, Bedford-Stuyvesant, Williamsburg. They can't stop it. It's out of control. Too many junkies and too much money. The Marine Corps couldn't stop it. The cops are a joke. They only play at it. Some of them are junkies."

The junkie says law enforcement in New York City is helpless to stop it. We don't know all the facts about the helplessness of the law elsewhere to control the drug traffic but if New York is helpless with all the policemen it has, can other places be any better off?

Only God can help. Only God can save America. Is America turning to God or away from God? Are we too far beyond the crossroads to turn back to God?

The Communist Plan to Destroy Churches

Secret documents seized during the liberation of Grenada from the communists have revealed the communist plan for dealing with churches everywhere, *including America.*

The Grenada Communist Ministry of the Interior had prepared a plan to first, enslave the churches and their congregations and preachers; second, to use them to brainwash the rest of the populace with communist propaganda; third, then destroy them when their usefulness to communism was over.

The document, called "Analysis of the Church in Grenada" was marked "Top Secret" by the communists and was among the many papers of the communist regime found by the U.S. forces that liberated Grenada. It said that all church leaders in Grenada — both laymen and clergy — were hostile to the revolution in various degrees. The communists know that Jesus Christ and His followers can never be reconciled with godless, Satanic communism whose God is the state.

Here is the communist plan for the church . . . not only in Grenada but everywhere:

1. Replace preachers and priests with what the communists call "sympathetic clergy," meaning communists posing as preachers and priests like they do in Russia where some people think there is still religious freedom because KGB agents in clerical robes staff the pulpits of the few officially sanctioned churches.

2. Replace all religious broadcasts with "progress reports" on communist projects.

3. Promote contacts among clergymen and laity with churchmen of other revolutionary countries linked to the theology of liberation, preaching the idea that a church must be committed to revolutionary positions.

4. Enroll all church leaders, clergy and laity, in political education courses, meaning communist propaganda courses.

5. Remove from both public and church schools all teachers and administrators considered to be deeply religious and

replace them with teachers considered more progressive, meaning more communist. This was a top education priority.

6. Open Marxist-Leninist bookshops in every church parish in the country, placing them in the churches themselves if necessary.

7. See to it that Marxist-Leninist literature is placed into the hands of every church member and every school child.

8. Step-up the monitoring of what preachers are saying in the pulpits and increase the surveillance of preachers in rural areas and any missionary activities in the country.

9. Introduce political education, meaning communist education, into Sunday School classes.

10. Open the movie theaters on Sunday mornings to compete with churches.

This basically was the communist plan for churches in Grenada, a plan for their enslavement, ultilization and then destruction.

This is what is going to happen — and what has always happened — when communism takes over a country. The biggest change is in the churches because the change involves their eventual destruction. The communists know Christ is their main enemy. They can change any government into a communist government, but they can't change a Christian into a communist or a Christian church into a communist party cell.

This is why Christian Crusade is so anti-communist—not just for political or economic reasons—but because of religious and spiritual reasons. People who don't think the fight against communism is very important are those who don't understand that communism is not just political and economic, it is Satanic and against God and His church.

The National Council of Churches Against America

The National Council of Churches sent a delegation to Soviet Russia to agree with the communists that America is to blame for world tension.

That's it! I'm fed up to here with the anti-American, pro-communist, Satanic tendencies of the Red National Council of Churches serving as a propaganda agent for the Kremlin.

A delegation 266 strong — or I should say 266 weak — went to Moscow about the same time the Soviets were boycotting the Olympic Games in Los Angeles. The press, as it usually does, called them American church leaders . . . but if they represent the true views and values of American church people, then the churches are in a lot worse trouble than I thought they were.

This bunch of alleged American church leaders turned immediately into communist followers as soon as they stepped onto Russian soil. They praised the Russian Orthodox Church clergy, which holds office at the pleasure of the Kremlin. They saw several hundred people in worship services and declared there was religious freedom in Russia — several hundred out of a population of millions, tens of thousands of whom are in communist jails and prisons for their Christian and Jewish religious beliefs.

The gall of this bunch of church council crazies to go over there and say there is religious freedom in Russia when the communist government specifically prohibits unlicensed church meetings and prohibits parents from teaching the Bible to their children and prohibits any church from ordaining an unlicensed minister.

The National Council of Churches is a communist propaganda agent. It supports communist revolutionaries throughout the world financially. It sends these big delegations to Moscow to make anti-American statements. It repeatedly supports known communists as head of its affiliate, the World Council of Churches and shares offices with the World Council in New York.

The reason many American churches and denominations are split today is because the National Council of Churches has divided them with not just liberalism in theology, but with downright support for socialism and communism and a perverted kind of religion that is little more than Marxist-Leninism being spoon-fed from the Kremlin.

A few Christian demonstrators in Moscow protested the National Council of Churches delegation but they were quickly removed by police and their fate is not known.

I wrote a book called *The Cross and the Sickle: Superchurch, the Infamous Story of the World-National Councils of Churches* and in its conclusion I said this, and I still say it today: "The National-World Councils of Churches are using the name of Christ in vain to advocate a godless system of Marxism for the world, a world that would be ruled by one super-government with a state-imposed church for all. The one-world state and church would not be run by the people or responsive to the people but would be run by political and ecclesiastical elitists, more concerned with their own power than with the power of the people and least concerned about the power of God."

The powers controlling the World and National Councils of Churches are Marxists marching under the banner of Christ.

Americans attending churches affiliated with the National-World Councils of Churches international conspiracy had better take a long careful look into the Bible and see if you can find any Biblical sanction for what the National and World Councils of Churches are doing supporting godless communism and liberation theology instead of the Gospel of Jesus Christ.

Methodists for Communism

The United Methodist Church, the largest financial supporter of the communist-oriented National Council of Churches, has passed a resolution calling for the United States to resume diplomatic relations with Fidel Castro's communist Cuba.

This is the Cuba that is **relaying** Soviet arms to the communist war in Central America, trying to overthrow the government of El Salvador. This is the Cuba that has allowed the Soviet Union to **re-install** missiles 90 miles from our shores without any hullabaloo like that which happened back in the 1960s. This is the Cuba that dumped all of its misfits and criminally insane and criminals and never-do-wells on our shores in 1980. Now let me say this, Cuba, that is, Castro, made some mistakes about some of those folks and some of them have turned out to be good Americans, although they are not citizens. One of them is a big league ballplayer now for Detroit . . . but many, many of them were **Castro castoffs** and they have had a hard time adjusting here in America, and among them were some out-and-out Castro **communist spies and subversives.** The so-called "Freedom Flotilla" simply overwhelmed the under-manned immigration and Naturalization Service responsible for screening them.

But back to the United Methodist Church and its pro-communist resolutions, decisions and inclinations. The United Methodists once again pulled the oldest trick out of the communist hat when they passed this resolution saying: "U.S. non-recognition of Cuba for the past 20 years has forced Cuba even closer to political and military reliance on the Soviet Union."

So what? Let them be closer. Who needs Castro and Cuba? We have lived 20 years or more without him and there is no reason to embrace him now. What we need to do is stay on guard against him and his communist allies sworn to overthrow our freedoms, including our religious freedoms.

The Methodist conferees said that Roman Catholic Bishops and several other unidentified Protestant denominations —

most of them in the National Council of Churches — have urged the **resumption of relations** with Castro's regime.

Let me tell you something. Throughout the history of this world, various organizations and individuals have urged the **resumption of relations with Satan** himself, but that's no reason why we should do it!

If we Christians did everything that the rest of the **worldly** are doing, we would no longer be Christians.

So far as the Roman Catholic Bishops are concerned, the United Methodists said that they joined them in **"rejecting deterrence** as a permanent basis for the securing and maintenance of peace."

I have news for them. The **ONLY** reason the United States has had peace here at home — within our 50 states — since World War II has been because of **deterrence**. And we have backed up **deterrence**, not just with nuclear weapons but with the blood of our foot soldiers and airmen and navy men in Korea and Vietnam and Lebanon — and yes, in Central America, too — to keep peace. The United Methodists, The Catholic Bishops (who have split their own church and who certainly can no longer be called majority leaders) and the National Council of Churches, are all **mistaken** about the power and strength of American deterrence. If our deterrence fails, they will be among the first to be **executed** as "enemies of the people," no matter their current propaganda usefulness.

All I can say is, God help us! We have these **big denominations** and **church councils** and **Catholic bishop leaders** calling for accommodation and appeasement with communist leaders who will condemn them and the rest of us to the firing squads the first chance they would get.

A Bishop Blames America

I never hesitate to speak up for America, even if it sometimes means speaking out against an alleged man of God.

But if a man of God jumps on America, and especially if he doesn't know what he is talking about, someone has to call his hand.

Not long ago in New York City, Bishop Paul Moore Jr., the bishop of the Episcopal Diocese in New York, delivered an **anti-American sermon** about Central America in which he said this, and I quote him:

"We Americans simply cannot go around the world shooting and killing innocent men, women and children as part of our national policy . . . we have brought violence and terrorism to Central America."

He went on to say that helping the anti-communist freedom fighters of Nicaragua in their fight against the communists who took over their country is **immoral** because, as the bishop puts it, "we commit murder without even the legal cloak of declared war."

The *New York Times* saw to it that the bishop's sermon was widely-circulated.

What I want to know, is where was the bishop when the communists were taking over Nicaragua in an undeclared war? What has the bishop had to say about the communists murdering innocent men, women and children in El Salvador and in Afghanistan and in Angola and in Southeast Asia? Where is a copy of the bishop's sermon against communist violence and terrorism when the communists shot down the South Korean airliner, killing 269 innocent people aboard. Now **THAT** was murder without even the legal cloak of a declared war, as the bishop likes to say.

And here is what I mean when I say he doesn't know what he is talking about, this Bishop Moore of New York. He went on to compare the Communist Sandinista government in Nicaragua with the early American government shortly after the Revolutionary War. He told his congregation that it took America 12 years to have an election after the revolution and that even then George Washington was the only candidate.

If I were not a minister of the Gospel myself, I might have something a lot stronger to say about that than BALONEY!

The early years of the United States were governed under the Articles of Confederation, and those articles made **no provision** for a president or a national election. When the Constitution was ratified and a president was to be elected, George Washington was the only candidate to receive votes from the **state electors**. The Constitution has been amended since then to provide for a popular vote, but Washington's election by electors chosen according to laws passed by state legislatures was perfectly legal and certainly far more democratic than the communist revolution that took Nicaragua by force.

I don't have to waste time teaching American history to Bishop Moore but he should know better than to twist it into an apology for communism from his pulpit.

The last time **Bishop Moore and his bunch of pro-communist apologists** campaigned for a surrender to communism, we got the collapse of Vietnam, the boat people and the slaughter of three million Cambodians by the North Vietnamese communist army. And that is very likely what would happen in El

61

Salvador if Bishop Moore and his pro-communist-sympathizing friends get their way in Central America.

I get sick of the muddle-headed, historically inaccurate and propaganda puffery of these **clerics and clergy** who refuse to believe or else are simply ignorant of the fact that communism is godless, that it is anti-religion, that they are playing into the hands of Marxist murderers with their **whining complaints** against America and adoring remarks about communism.

El Salvador is not perfect and neither is America, but both are much further along the road to freedom and human rights and human dignity than communist-controlled Nicaragua, which is nothing more than a puppet on the string of Cuba and the Soviet Union.

U.S. Government vs. the Churches

It's bad enough that the communists have a plan for destroying the churches without the United States government trying to do the same thing!

Government is waging open warfare against the churches of America, having jailed seven Christians in Nebraska and also having ordered that churches start paying social security taxes for all employees.

The seven Nebraskans are fathers of children who have been attending a Christian school in Louisville, Nebraska, which state authorities claim doesn't meet the state's education standards. The Nebraska men believe the school they support is better than the godless state schools where no prayer or Bible reading is allowed.

According to the Nebraska state constitution, there should be no charges at all against these men. It says: "It shall be the duty of the legislature to pass suitable laws to protect every religious denomination in the peaceable enjoyment of its own mode of public worship and to encourage schools and the means of instruction."

Did you get that? "**encourage schools and the means of instruction.**" Of course, that was written before the U.S. Supreme Court began meddling with education and telling everyone what was good and what was not good for their children. The Supreme Court decided God is not good, the Bible is not good and prayer is not good so all of them were thrown out of the schools. If anyone argues with that . . . like the seven men in Nebraska . . . they're thrown in jail!

As for the Social Security issue, the federal government for the first time in history has imposed a direct tax on churches and church schools starting January 1, 1984, by including all churches in the social security system. In the past, social security has been optional for churches and the fact is that about 80 per cent of all American church organizations participated in it voluntarily, but now the government is forcing the other 20 per cent in and raising the tax — they call it contributions — by seven per cent on the part of the churches. The government then makes the churches **tax collectors** for the government by authorizing them to collect a seven per cent increase from church workers.

This knocks the wall of separation of church and state as flat as a picket fence hit by a tornado. Some 5,000 pastors have said they are going to resist the Social Security requirement and announced they are prepared to go to jail in protest if necessary.

What is this country coming to when Nebraska Baptists are jailed for trying to educate their children as Christians and 5,000 preachers are prepared to go to jail to maintain the integrity of church and state separation?

The government is guilty of failing to reform Social Security and instead is patching together a bunch of petty regulations and higher taxes to bail out the system. Instead of offering Americans a choice of voluntary private retirement-saving options, the government has **nailed to the cross of Social Security the church workers of America,** including the preachers!

Now when the big banks and bankers protested to Washington about the mandatory withholding of taxes on dividends last year, Congress backed down and changed the law. Will Congress back down when Christians protest, or will it stand idly by while 5,000 preachers go to jail along with the fathers in Nebraska who want a Christian education for their children?

The government is pushing the Christians of this country into a corner and won't stop pushing until there is some resistance. The government took prayer and Bible reading out of the schools and nothing has been done about it. . .Now government is putting men in jail for supporting Christian education. Now government is forcing new and higher social security taxes on churches, in effect **regulating church business** for the first time in American history. What next? When does the government man come around and tell the preachers what to preach? When does the government padlock the doors of the churches that don't go along with everything the government demands? When do Christian people and long-silent Christian leaders speak up against this kind of government abuse of churches and church people? Or are we expected to go along like sheep to the coming government slaughter of religion in America?

Make no mistake about it, religious liberty in America is being threatened by the government. The liberal, national news media tried to make a big deal in the recent election campaign about religion taking over government but the fact is that government is trying to take over religion.

Here are some examples, as opposed to media myths:

1. A church in Oklahoma was sued because it dared to discipline — according to their church doctrine — one of its members who made a self-declaration of her sin.

2. The National Labor Relations Board is trying to take over jurisdiction of some of the employees of the Roman Catholic Archdiocese of Chicago.

3. The federal government won its suit in the Bob Jones University case to limit tax exemptions for religious organizations that disagree with Supreme Court and congressional decisions on moral issues.

4. The Internal Revenue Service is making a series of arbitary and burdensome audits of many church and Christian organizations.

5. In light of recent Supreme decisions, Catholic and certain other religious institutions are being threatened with loss of tax-exemptions because their refusal to ordain women is viewed by the government as sex discrimination.

6. Recent tax cases brought by the Internal Revenue Service threaten the freedom of religious groups to raise funds, to speak out in favor of legislation on their behalf, and to have leaders hold money in trust for members.

But the most controversial of all church-state relations is in the field of education where the government has set itself up as the only or at least the superior educator for society, including the government belief that prayer and Bible reading have no place in education. The government is making things extremely hard for Christians who want to start their own schools and who believe tuition tax-credits should be government policy, relieving Christian and private school supporters of double taxation to support public schools not attended by their children.

Church members have been harrassed and threatened by government agents and law enforcement authorities for trying to educate their children in their homes where they can teach Christian values and Bible truths. In Nebraska, church leaders and pastors were arrested and thrown in jail for operating a church school which Nebraska education authorities claimed did not meet state standards.

The government was the first aggressor in denying prayer and Bible reading in the public schools. Now churches have become aggressive in asserting their rights to educate the children of church members in religious values. Government and churches are bumping into each other and the government has the power of existing laws, of making new laws and of finally ruling through the courts what laws are to be enforced. The churches and religious organizations must rely on the power of prayer and the power of God to help them and they also have civil rights as citizens to work for laws on their behalf. They should not be threatened by the IRS, the tax arm of the government, with punishment for exercising their constitutional rights as citizens.

Not all government officials are anti-religion. Terry Eastland, a special assistant to the U.S. Attorney, went on record as saying: "Christians have the most serious reservations about public schools. Religion is too often treated as if it were bad for the health."

Christians must continue to support this fight for their rights, for their constitutional tax exemptions, for the education of their children as they see fit in light of their religion, and for those speaking out on their behalf.

It is not religion that is trying to take over government in America, as some recent candidates for high office and the national news media would have us believe, it is government trying to take over religion.

And the Walls Come Tumbling Down

Just like the wall of Jericho at the sound of Joshua's trumpets, the alleged "wall of separation" between church and state has begun to tumble down since the Pawtucket, Rhode Island, nativity scene case.

The leftist, liberal news media and the humanist politicians and organizations have kept what they call a "low profile" on that decision by the Supreme Court but the fact is that the case — on full reading — has a tremendous impact on church-state association, not separation.

First, there is no wording in the Constitution separating church and state. The news media and the humanists have been using that term as propaganda, but it's just not there and the Supreme Court knows it and now has said as much. The First Amendment says: "Congress shall make no law respecting an establishment of religion, or prohibiting the free exercise thereof . . ."

The amendment restricts **Congress,** not the states, and the states' subsidiaries, the cities, from establishing religions or prohibiting their exercise. In the 1940s, the Supreme Court construed the Fourteenth Amendment — some 70 years after it was passed — to extend the First Amendment wording to the states as well as Congress.

But now, the Supreme Court construes it the other way and says the city of Pawtucket, Rhode Island, cannot be prohibited from setting up a nativity scene because, in the words of the court's chief justice Warren Burger: "To forbid its use would be a stilted overreaction contrary to our history and our holdings."

The chief justice also said something else very, very important in ruling in favor of the nativity scene: "The Constitution does not require a complete separation of church and state; contrariwise, it affirmatively mandates accommodation, not merely toleration, of all religion, and forbids hostility toward any."

This says that the government not only must tolerate religion but must accommodate it. In other words, the government's agencies and bureaus such as the Internal Revenue Service and various police and zoning agencies of local governments must not only tolerate churches but in fact are under obligation by the Supreme Court to accommodate them!

Not all the court agreed, but the dissenters were in a minority. Justice Brennan called the nativity scene "insulting to those who insist for religious or personal reasons that the story of Christ is in no sense a part of history nor an unavoidable element of our national heritage."

No matter what Justice Brennan says, Christ is a part of our national history and heritage, whether he or anyone else likes it or not. God is mentioned specifically in the Declaration of Independence. The President takes his oath of office with his hand on the Bible. "In God We Trust" is on our coins. Thanksgiving Day is a national holiday, as is Christmas. God is in the pledge of allegiance. Chaplains are employed by the armed forces. Congress opens each session with a prayer. Christians have been at the heart and the center of this nation's government leadership and national development throughout its history.

Government, in fact, is of God. Paul's inspired words in I Corinthians 12:28 says: "*And God hath set some in the church: first apostles, second prophets, third teachers; after the miracles, then gifts of healing, helps, governments, diversities of tongues.*"

Without God, there would be no government. Communism is not a government. Dictatorships are not government. God's government is for God's people, not for one-man glorification or for Satanic use to tyranize and kill. In America, we need to pray for our leaders, whoever they are when we have elected them, pray that God provides them with the wisdom to govern justly. Prayer sustains — and America and prayer are of God. There can be no alleged separation of church and state in America if America is to survive.

The Rise of Pornography

When a nation starts to lose its sense of values, turn away from God, embrace the things of Satan, sees church attendance wane and decline, fails to give to God's work on earth — when all those things start happening in a country, one of the early symptoms of its decadence and corruption is the rise of pornography.

The pornography industry is booming in America. Untold millions of people in this country are sick, requiring daily or weekly injections of pornography, and organized crime controlling the industry is reaping millions of dollars from it.

Los Angeles is a porno production headquarters and Atlanta is a national distribution center for pornography. Nearly every local police raid on pornographic distribution centers reveals records linking the local pornographers with Atlanta, which in turn get most of the production from Los Angeles. That's what was revealed in Tulsa, Oklahoma, not long ago when police raided a porno warehouse.

Here are some facts about the pornography industry that is undermining the moral values of America and corrupting not only the sick adults who support it but also thousands of young children forced to participate in this Satanic work:

SALES — About $6 billion in annual pornographic sales, if you include such sickos as Playboy, Hustler, Playgirl, Gallery, High Society and dozens of other sick magazines passing themselves off as entertainment and good reading. There is reason to believe from police raids and confiscated evidence throughout the country that up to $4 billion annually being invested in the production of pornography is money being laundered by organized crime from such sources as drugs, gambling, prostitution and robbery.

PRODUCTION — A sleazy outfit calling itself the Adult Film Association of America, working out of Los Angeles and other places, produces nearly all pornography, filming endlessly, then editing the tapes for reproduction in video cassettes, adult magazines, still photographs, the cable television industry and so-called "adult" bookstores.

CHILD PORNOGRAPHY — The pornography syndicates "farm out" the more dangerous child pornography filming to independents to reduce risk for the organized crime syndicates.Some 100,000 children in America are believed to be used as prostitutes and are being molested by professional pornographic child molestors on behalf of the porn industry.

RETAIL OUTLETS — Pornography is not only being distributed by adult bookstores and theaters, porn magazines and x-rated cable television networks, the slick magazines are available in thousands of convenience stores and drug stores throughout America.

The porno kings are making so much money that they are making plans to buy major Hollywood studios along with all their facilities and the contract stars who will be willing to go along with porno movie making for general distribution. They are financing the openings of more and more adult bookstores and theaters, entering the publishing field (protected by the First Amendment, of course), with more porn magazines and producing more video cassettes for home television sets. In the works are movies about topless Las Vegas reviews, nudist beaches, nudist colonies and for cable television subscription channels like Playboy Channel, Pleasure Channel and ON-TV — nudist soap operas are in production.

Christians must demand a return to decency in this country. What is being done in your town about the porno industry? Are you hearing any sermons from the pulpit against it, demanding action by authorities? Are any Christians in your town up in arms against the spread of pornography and its demoralizing influence? Is the Congressman in your district aware of the porno industry in his home neighborhood? Christians should be finding these things out and demanding that a stop be put to porn and child molestation for porn in each and every city in America.

We don't always have to go to the overseas mission field to find lost souls — there are plenty right here in America where the field is ripe unto harvest, but the laborers are still few.

U.S. Surgeon General Everett C. Koop says that viewing pornography and violence on television and in the movies can be as dangerous to your mental health as smoking is to your physical health.

Dr. Koop attended a symposium on Media Violence and Pornography in Toronto and was a panelist who agreed that excessive viewing of violence in movies and TV has negative effects on mental health.

Getting down to cases, **the panel** condemned the following popular American television programs (which are also seen in Canada), movies and rock music video programming, such as:

"Magnum P.I." despite the nice-guy image of leading actor Tom Selleck; The A-Team," "The Fall Guy," "T.J. Hooker," "Hardcastle and McCormick," "Knight Rider," and the violent words in "Dallas" and "Dynasty," along with violent words and action in "Mike Hammer."

Movies they condemned included "Scarface," "The Texas Chainsaw Massacre," "Toolbox Murders," "Vice Squad" and "I Spit On Your Grave."

Rock star Michael Jackson, the current idol of many American youngsters, was criticized for his rock video rendition of "Thriller," which shows an attractive young man enjoying terrorizing his girl friend.

Other harmful video programs identified by the panel include "Under Cover of the Night" by The Rolling Stones, which shows a lot of automatic-weapons violence and a lawless execution and "Dancing With Myself," featuring a naked women struggling in chains behind a translucent sheet.

The point is that if you are receiving rock video programming over television in your home, you better take a look at some of it to see if you want that kind of show in your house for your kids. One rock outfit called "Kansas" shows film of a woman supposedly being burned alive to the sound of heavy rock music. I'm not suggesting you watch all this, only that you decide if this is what you want for your kids on TV.

Dr. Koop, the U.S. Surgeon General, is considered to be an old fuddy-duddy by militant women who don't like his stand against abortion, and now he has come out against pornography in movies and television to bring down the wrath of the TV networks and Hollywood on his head.

Dr. Koop is a man of great courage. He doesn't flow along with the popular tide of what seems to pass for culture in America today. He is NOT the **Doctor of Trend** or Fashion in America because he stands up for such old-fashioned things as virtue, decent behavior, morality and Godliness. He is hated by the liberals who run Hollywood and TV.

But men like Dr. Koop are not so interested in what his enemies think of him as he is in trying to save the young people of America from evil and sin.

It is popular nowdays to show evil and sin as acceptable and even fun on television and in Hollywood movies. Anything goes! What right does Dr. Koop have to tell people they shouldn't enjoy a little evil and sin in entertainment?

He has the same right of free speech as the producers and purveyors of pornography do under their idea of freedom of the press to present pornography and violence in TV and movies. If they choose to do that, they open themselves to criticism from Dr. Koop and all other decent Americans who believe like he does that pornography and violence weaken the morality of our nation and corrupt citizens who view it and condone it, thereby threatening the well-being and security of all of us.

Dr. Koop is a Christian. That's why he's not popular with the purveyors of pornography. He has a duty not only as U.S. Surgeon General but also a Christian to stand up for his principles and his convictions. America is still blessed to have some good men like Dr. Koop in high office who are unafraid to speak out against Satan and his handymen who are trying to flood America with pornography, violence, illicit sex and sin.

God's Plague on American Spiritual Weakness:
Herpes and AIDS

God has brought down a plague on American sodomites in the form of an incurable disease that is killing them off at a rate of up to 75 per cent of all who are stricken.

The disease has baffled medical science. It takes several forms—virus, cancer, pneumonia, failure of disease immunity that is fatal.

It is called Acquired Immunity Deficiency Syndrome, abbreviated AIDS. One of its most feared forms is called Kaposi's Sarcoma, KS, a cancer.

The KS cancer is a member of the same herpes family or viruses that cause cold sores and genital herpes infection.

So far only hundreds have died but the death toll will go into the thousands this year.

It has the American homosexual "community" in a panic and has put a brake on the so-called sexual revolution of promiscuous lifestyles for fear of contracting the disease from casual bisexual bed partners.

"AND HE BROKE DOWN THE HOUSES OF THE SODOMITES..." -II Kings 23:7

The sex disease epidemic that first alarmed health officials months ago has now spread to a new group of victims — infants and young children whose own immunity to contagious diseases is not fully developed. They contract it from child molestation by those infected and also by having been born in families where one other person was in close contact with what scientists call a "risk factor," meaning either a homosexual man or a drug addict who picked up the disease by means of an

70

unsanitary needle used by someone already infected.

"For their vine is the vine of Sodom, and the fields of Gomorrah: their grapes are grapes of gall, their clusters are bitter." -Jeremiah 32:32

The death rate among known victims who have contracted the disease so far is 38 per cent but when researchers look at those victims who were diagnosed only a year or more ago, they find the death rate is closer to 60 per cent, meaning that many people now living who have the disease are doomed to die soon. The two-year survival rate of patients with Kaposi's Sarcoma, the cancer, is only 25 per cent, meaning **75 per cent die within two years of contracting it!**

"Thy terribleness hath deceived thee, and the pride of thine heart . . . I will bring thee down . . . as in the overthrow of Sodom and Gomorrah . . . no man shall abide there, neither shall a Son of Man dwell in it." -Jeremiah 49:16-18

Scientists and researchers in dozens of government and university laboratories are considering the possibility that the disease is caused by a new mutant virus. But to isolate such a virus is an arduous, costly, and time-consuming task. Meanwhile, the caseload and the death toll keep rising.

"The cry of Sodom and Gomorrah is great because their sin is grievous . . ." -Genesis 18:20

Investigators of the AIDS Task Force, a special arm of the national Center for Disease Control in Atlanta, report that the disease is principally a phenonmenon of what they call the "raunchy subculture in large cities, where bars and bathhouses are literal hotbeds of sexual and homosexual promiscuity." They say the major cities where the disease is becoming rampant, and where AIDS information centers have been established are New York, San Francisco, Atlanta, Philadelphia, Houston and Miami.

"And their dead bodies shall lie in the street of the great city, which spiritually is called Sodom . . ." -Revelation 11:8

The plague is spreading beyond the large cities and is appearing in smaller towns as the epidemic spreads. For example, the Joplin Globe newspaper in Joplin, Mo., reported on its front page on December 5, 1982 that the "disease known as AIDS that often leads to fatal complications has appeared in Joplin." And Joplin is not the only town concerned about this tragic medical phenomenon. Similar reports are popping up in local newspapers throughout the country as the press brings this "closet" disease to public attention.

"But I say unto you that it shall be more tolerable in that day for Sodom, than for that city." -Luke 10:12

71

The AIDS task force investigators report that an individual's level of "sexual activity is highly significant." Dr. Harold Jaffee, assistant director of the task force, says data from his study revealed that a common trait among victims was they that had a large number of sex partners, sometimes more than 60 in a year, or an average of more than one a week. Some already had a history of the more common venereal diseases such as syphilis and gonorrhea. But doctors say syphilis and gonorrhea can be controlled, treated and usually cured while the AIDS ailment runs rampant.

Common symptoms include recurrent fevers, swollen lymph glands, loss of weight and appitite and a general "rundown" feeling. The symptoms worsen over a matter of weeks and months.

"Then The Lord rained upon Sodom and Gomorrah• brimstone and fire from the Lord out of Heaven." -Genesis 19:24

The homosexuals and sodomites who misnamed themselves "gays" are not so happy now. Many have come to fear any sexual contact after having seen friends or "lovers" die horrible deaths. Some who have contracted the incurable disease have committed suicide. The "gay" looks have turned to gray looks.

"The show of their countenance doth witness against them: and they declare their sin as Sodom, they hide it not. Woe unto their soul! For they have rewarded evil unto themselves."

-Isaiah 3:9

In their panic, the sodomites are rushing to cooperate with medical researchers. They are holding medical fund raising events and in some places haved raised as much as $100,000 for patient services, community education and research on AIDS. Periodicals catering to homosexuals have begun publishing articles about the outbreak. The Gay Men's Health Crisis, founded in January, 1982, has raised and awarded some $30,000 for research grants and has established a 24-hour national telephone "hot line" to advise those who have contracted the disease about finding medical attention, although doctors have been unable to cure them.

"And they took all the goods of Sodom and Gomorrah, and all their victuals, and went their way." -Genesis 14:11

Trying to trace the origins of the disease, researchers believe the original strain of herpes came from Africa in past centuries. More recently, the disease was traced to the "gay" communities of New York and San Francisco and Los Angeles, where victims tended to be white, middle class, highly promiscuous with male sex partners and some are bisexual.

"But the men of Sodom were wicked and sinners before the Lord Exceedingly." -Genesis 13:13

Then a disconcerting connection turned up when a host of Haitian immigrants in Miami, Florida, began reporting having contracted the disease. The death rate among Haitians, who generally were in poorer health and physical condition, was appalling. Dr. Alvin Friedman-Kien, a New York University dermatologist with considerable experience in AIDS and KS research, told the press that the New York "gay" connection with Haitians has been well-known for years in the homosexual subculture.

He said that New York City "gays" had been vacationing in Haiti many years because of the availability of cheap male sex there. Average daily wages in Haiti range from $1.50 to $2.50 and the New York "gays" were willing to pay more than a day's wages for a single sex experience. Word got around and untold numbers of New York "gays" flew to Haiti for their vacations, taking the disease back to New York with them and spreading it around. Soon many were in their death throes.

"Behold, this was the iniquity of thy sister Sodom, pride, fulness of bread and abundance of idleness. . .They were haughty and committed abomination before Me; therefore I took them away as I saw good." -Exekiel 16:49-50

Victims who don't get cancer from the disease nevertheless contract raging infections from bacteria, viruses and other micro-organisms that hardly ever cause serious disease in healthy bodies, but because this new sex disease breaks down the immunity factor in those stricken, they can fall seriously ill, even developing pneumonia from a common cold. Among these kinds of victims, 47 per cent have died. Among those with both cancer and the uncontrollable infections, the death rate has been a steady 68 per cent, ranging up to 75 per cent in some study areas, most dying in a debilitating fever.

"Even as Sodom and Gomorrah. . .Giving themselves over to fornication, and going after strange flesh, are set forth for an example, suffering the vengeance of eternal fire. -Jude 7

So the misnamed "gay" life has gone sour for the sodomites. And it has had a tremendous impact on the "swinging singles" lifestyle, featuring nightly "pickups" of heterosexual partners (opposite sexes) in singles bars or at social gatherings for one-night liaisons. People who rebelled in the sex revolution against conventional morality and Biblical direction and instruction called it "Dolce Vita," or "the sweet life." Everyone could "do their own thing" and have free sex with many partners without any "hangups" or guilt feelings. But now AIDS and KS, the plague of the Sodomites is burrowing into even the heterosexual life as it turns out that many a man or woman is bisexual and has contracted the plague from homosexual or lesbian encounters.

". . .The glory of kingdoms, the beauty of Chaldees' excellency, shall be as when God overthrew Sodom and Gomorrah."
-Isaiah 13:19

The bad news for the sad "gays" is that the plague is gaining ground despite the efforts of medical science to find a cure. At present there is no serum, no pill, no medicine, no nostrum that will cure or even curb the relentless spread of the new sex disease from person to person and then within the body. The "gay" life and the promiscuous sexual lifestyle — the "alternate lifestyle" as the press often so politely phrases it — is now tumbled down in the wake of this plague.

"And Lot lifted up his eyes, and beheld all the Plain of Jordan, that it was well watered everywhere, before the Lord destroyed Sodom and Gomorrah. . ." -Genesis 13:10

The cure is found in the Bible: sexual chastity and mutual faith between married man and wife. The only way to be assured of avoiding this sexual plague is to remain a virgin until marriage, marry a virgin, and then each be faithful to the other eternally. As for homosexuals now living in fear but who have not yet contracted the disease, their safest path is repentance. The Bible offers them this advice:

"Hear the word of the Lord, the rulers of Sodom; give ear unto the law of our God, ye people of Gomorrah. . .wash you, make you clean: put away the evil of your doings from before Mine eyes: cease to do evil." Isaiah 1:10-16

Whatever Happened to Bible Mothers?

A woman was nominated for vice president and a woman will be nominated for president someday soon and all this may or may not be good for America. But one thing it is doing is prompting a reappraisal of women in America . . . and in the world.

American women are the most fortunate in the world. They should thank God every day they don't live in Iran under Muslim restriction . . . they should thank Christ for that. It was He who began women's liberation, not Gloria Stienhem or Bella Abzug or Geraldine Ferraro-Zaccaro.

Now that so many women think they are "free," they make the mistake of thinking they are free from God as well as free from man. They may be free from man on this earth but they are not free from God, and when they learn that, and take another look at God's Word through the Bible, they will see that the cost of what they think is freedom may not be worth the womanhood lost.

Humanism has taught the so-called modern woman that she can find fulfillment in education, career, independence, selfcenterdness and materialism. Subordinating themselves to a husband and the responsibility of children is thought to be demeaning. Old-fashioned grandmothers and mothers are in short supply and few are the American children today who have them to enjoy. Singleness, divorce and lesbianism run rampant in America these days.

And yet . . . there are young women coming into the churches of America today, entering into the body of Christ, confessing and proclaiming that all of these modern-day, worldly deviations have failed to bring what they thought would be their promised rewards.

They are finding that there is more joy and fulfillment in the high calling of God for women to be wives and mothers. Homes and families are oasis of peace and love in a troubled world.

Believe it or not, many women have found that the economic sacrifice of staying home with children instead of going out to work and leaving the kids for someone else to raise returns more rewards later in life than any material or economic rewards received in the short-term by the working mother.

It boils down to whether financial reward is more important than children being loved and properly reared. A nation that is killing 1.5 million unborn children a year by abortion and yet has so many working women in the marketplace contributing to economic wealth and pleasure certainly calls our nation's priorities into question.

There is a ministry for women in the Bible and it is stated clearly in Titus 2:4, which says: *"That they may teach the young women to be sober, to love their husbands, to love their children."*

Is that too much to ask of a woman? To be sober, or sober-minded, to love her husband and to love her children.

America could not have been what it is today, still the greatest country on earth, had it not been for that Titus 2:4 ministry of millions upon millions of American women who remained sober and loved their husbands and loved their children. The family women of America have always been the true strength of America. We men would make a worse mess of things than we do if it were not for the Titus 2:4 ministry of the women of America who have stood for the Bible, stood for the church, stood for Christ, stood for God, stood for sober-mindedness, loved their husbands, and loved their children.

Thank God for them and their example may save America yet!

The ERA is dead again but women's liberation lives on.

The Equal Rights Amendment for women has failed repeatedly and looks dead as a doornail, but women's liberation is alive and growing though not healthy.

I don't mean it's unpopular — far from it — all I mean is that it may not be as good for women, or for men, as the feminist radicals who promote it would have us think.

One of the big troubles with women's liberation is that it has also liberated many men from what used to be conventional responsibilities. And women don't like that. And a lot of men are not so sure they like their so-called "new freedom" very much either.

If you ever watch any of this continuing debate about "women's lib" or the "new sexual freedoms" on television — which has become the national debate forum — then you see what I mean. The women who fight for women's lib on television are usually highly-educated, successful career women. But they hardly ever laugh. They are always so serious. They are usually downright hostile. And the fact is, off camera when the public isn't looking at them, they are in many cases sad and unhappy and can be very mean.

They like to call men "wimps" without knowing quite what they mean by that. But I know what they mean. They mean unmanliness. You see, a lot of men found freedom from the responsibility of careers and breadwinning and families when a lot of women embraced women's lib. And the result is that neither the women or the men are happy.

What this all means is that these people — men and women both — who have thrown off the Scriptural responsibilities set out for both men and women by the Bible are now relying on themselves instead of God.

And that's what's making them sick and unhappy. They become swamped in too much vanity, too much self-preoccupation, too much fear and uncertainty about whether or not they are truly capable of making the right decisions in their lives without God's help and guidance.

When liberated men and women give themselves over to free sex without responsibility or affection or love, when it becomes just another animal-like act in life without romance or heartfelt care, then it loses its value. And those who partake in it feel in their hearts that they lose their own value as well.

It is no accident that men with wives and families tend to

lead **happier lives,** earn and save more money, go to church and give more to God's work, than do men who have been liberated from such responsibilities by women's lib, **which also means men's lib.**

Fathers who do not support their children are too often told that it is society's responsibility to support them, that their own primary responsibility is to themselves first. This is the so-called "me first generation" kind of thinking . . . me first everyone else next or last.

Ant that's why it is sick. And that's why the women and the men involved in this phony liberation and sexual freedom movement are sick at heart and mind. They are trying to run their own lives without God and without His Word, the Bible.

Jesus tells us to love one another. He loved you and me so much He gave His life for us. Now **THAT'S** responsibility. Love is not free. It carries with it responsibility . . . responsibility to God, responsibility to the one who is loved, responsibility to the offspring of that love, and responsibility to one's self.

None of that is free. None of that is "liberated" from responsibility. None of that is radically different from the precepts of the Bible that tell us about love and life and family relationships.

The fact is that no one is truly "liberated." If you throw God and His rules out of your life in the name of "liberation," then you fall into Satan's trap. No wonder so many liberated people are sick and scared and unhappy with what they think is their new freedom. What has happened is that they have lost their freedom and fallen into the oldest bondage of all — sin and death through Satan instead of life and freedom through Christ.

The liberal, leftist national news media goes out of its way to find women activists from the old ERA crowd to attack President Reagan for being insensitive to women. They call it the "gender gap."

Well, let's look at Reagan's record on issues important to women and we will see that the "gender gap" is phony, made up by the women activists and the news media.

1. President Reagan has come out openly against abortion and the ERA. Nothing else he does for women—and we will look at that in just a moment—makes any difference to the news media or the ERA and *abortion-on-demand* crowd. They will be forever against him because of that. But the president knows that most Americans have some serious reservations about abortion and that the ERA died in 1982, was resurrect-

ed in Congress briefly in 1983 before dying again for lack of support. So President Reagan is not alone in America when he stands against abortion and against the ERA.

2. President Reagan is the first president to have three women in his cabinet; the first president to appoint a woman to the Supreme Court, and Justice Sandra Day O'Connor is outstanding; he is the first president to appoint a woman ambassador to the United Nations and Jean Kirkpatrick stood up to bullying of Soviet Russia and its stooges there better than any ambassador to the U.N. we've ever had. She is stronger than many men on anti-communism.

3. President Reagan has appointed 1,187 women to full and part-time positions in the federal government, believed to be a record since records on such appointments are incomplete.

4. President Reagan has supported the Economic Recovery Act, which includes a measure to decrease the tax burden on working wives and increase tax credits for working mothers, something the ERA never advocated.

5. President Reagan supported a measure in 1982 that allows state courts to divide equally military pension payments between a husband who served in the service and his wife, in the event they get divorced.

6. President Reagan is supporting legislation which, if adopted by Congress, would reward states with money bonuses for collecting support from absent fathers of both welfare and non-welfare families. The bill also calls for mandatory deductions from wages when support payment delinquencies occur. The federal government is now spending millions on aid to dependent children and this new proposal would try to reduce this by rewarding states for law enforcement concerning abandoned families.

7. President Reagan is supporting Social Security changes that would provide more benefits for disabled widows and divorced women.

8. President Reagan has appointed The White House Working Group on Women to monitor issues of importance to the women of America and suggest to him any legislation the group believes should be called to his attention.

The record shows the president has done more for women than President Jimmy Carter, but because Carter supported the ERA and was non-commital on abortion, the liberals call Reagan insensitive to women.

President Reagan has not offended most women in America but he has made enemies of women who want abortion on demand who don't think parents have a right to know if their teen-age daughters are receiving contraceptive materials and who, through the ERA, would have junked many laws that protect the rights of women.

President Reagan has made his share of mistakes . . . every president does. And he, just as any other president, can't please everybody all the time, but the record shows he is getting an undeserved rap from women activists and the news media because his conscience and his high morals won't permit him to give in to their liberal demands.

Putting Down America

Every school year, one of the big things on American university campuses is to hold symposiums about what's wrong with America and how bad it is going to be in the year 2000.

Since 1984 did not turn out to be what George Orwell predicted, the emphasis has shifted to the year 2000. Here in America, at least, we are still free from the kind of Big Brother communism they have in Russia and all the other Marxist states. So the symposium speakers this year have focused on the year 2000.

These speakers are liberal, leftist academic experts on everything from the ecology to the economy, from political science to pathology. And most of them have been saying about the same thing to middle-class college kids from Omaha and Topeka and Peoria and Sioux City and Terre Haute — that is, something like this: "America is a dead, life-denying society". . or. . ."I'm not certain it will be a good thing to be alive in America in the year 2000". . .or. . ."America is a country run by 60 families and 180 corporations who control 95 per cent of the wealth". . .or. . ."Due to the sharp drop in the Gross National Product, the thin veneer of freedom in America is no longer possible." That kind of stuff.

The radicals saying all that are men and women in their 30s and 40s and even 50s who have studied under radical professors and who are now professors or Ph.D.s of some sort themselves.

They paint these gloomy pictures to auditoriums full of kids wearing designer jeans who worry more about where to find a place to park their car on the campus than they do about the gross national product or who controls all that wealth they are spending going to college.

Part of the blame for this mad scene — liberal professors wearing gold chains around their necks and diamond rings on their fingers and custom-made loafers on their feet talking to college kids already richer than most people in the world about what a sorry place America is today and will be in the year 2000 — part of the blame for such madness must be placed on the liberal, leftist national American news media that spends most of its resources looking for and broadcasting **bad news**.

Today's young journalists are nearly all products of these same kinds of professors. . .admirers of Marxism, or if not admirers, at least too "dispassionate" — as they put it — to stand up against Marxism. Many of these journalists today like to **ride a high horse** of what they call "professionalism," which means report what communism is doing without criticizing it. To criticize communism wouldn't be "professional." To criticize America **IS** "professional." It's a double standard that Moscow itself couldn't have set up any better.

My guess is that most of the kids from Omaha and Peoria and the other middle-class towns of mid-America will go back there or to bigger cities and settle into middle-class lives themselves, all the while criticizing America but living very well while doing it.

The godless schools of this country have been allowing this to happen for the past 20 years since prayer and Bible-reading and moral guidance were thrown out the window. If the Bible were still in the schools, these kids and some of these Doctors of Marxist Trend would have learned from it that moral and spiritual values historically have under-girded the material wealth of individuals and societies in Western Civilization.

The reason that communism-Marxism is spiritually bankrupt today is that it banned God, too, 45 years before American schools banished God from the classroom. So agents of Satan in many gold-chain disguises have filled the vacuum of God's withdrawal and have been undermining American values — and American kids — ever since.

America was founded on the Christian principles of moral and spiritual values but has been seduced by the narrow doctrines of political economy in recent years.

Chapter 4

WHATEVER HAPPENED TO THE MONROE DOCTRINE?

In addition to avoiding the pitfall of Latin American style socialism — if it's not too late already — America needs to reinstate the Monroe Doctrine.

Whatever happened to the Monroe Doctrine anyway? It's not really been used since Castro turned Cuba into a Soviet fortress in the 1960s after the Kennedy-Khruschev missile crisis. Since then it has been trampled underfoot by communist aggression in Latin America.

(I must warn you that the following chapters will be difficult to digest, unless they are read slowly and prayerfully. Indeed, these remaining chapters are probably the most important part of the book, for they deal with the present "COMMUNIST ENCIRCLEMENT" of the United States.

Most of the facts and statistics are taken from official U.S. Government documents, primarily the "U.S. Congressional Record."

So, you are about to be exposed to sobering facts and the resulting obvious conclusions that demand an answer from "we, the people of the United States" to this question: "A COMMUNIST AMERICA: MUST IT BE?" Action or apathy on our part will dictate the answer.)

At any rate, about the last time the Monroe Doctrine was heard from was during the Kennedy-Khruschev missile crisis in the early 1960s when it was mentioned during their negotiations to get Soviet offensive missiles out of Cuba. Since then it has been ignored by both Moscow and Washington. The missiles are back along with much more in Cuba — airfields, naval bases, planes, ships, brigades of troops, droves of "technical advisers" and a regular supply and communications system to maintain all of it.

Kennedy and Khruschev reached an agreement, in writing, to settle the missile crisis. Over the years the Soviets have broken that agreement repeatedly. Here are some of the major violations of the "understanding" established by the then two leaders of the world's great superpowers:

• The Soviets built a strategic submarine base at Cienfuegos, complete with a nuclear warhead handling facility.

• The Soviets have sent submarines of the Gulf and Echo class to Cienfuegos, all armed with strategic nuclear warhead-equipped, long-range missiles.

• The Soviet TU-95 Bear heavy bomber flies regular missions to Cuba, often passing nearby the East Coast of the United States.

• The Soviets are shipping more than 66,000 tons of military equipment annually to Cuba, three times the amount shipped there in 1962 before the Kennedy-Khruschev "understanding" was reached.

• The Soviets have stationed a combat brigade of more than 4,000 soldiers in Cuba.

• The Soviets have sent a nuclear missile-equipped naval task force on a Caribbean tour, threatening vital oilfields in Latin America as well as coastal and offshore oil supplies in the United States. Such a task force is not conducive to peaceful cargo and oil shipments in the Gulf of Mexico.

All of these are clear-cut violations of the Kennedy-Khruschev agreement, to say nothing of the Monroe Doctrine.

The British policy and position in the Falklands pales in comparison.

The liberal national news media in the United States practically ignored the 1985 meeting of the 14th General Assembly of the Organization of American States at which the Cuban exiles presented the following information based on intelligence sources and their own informants within Cuba:

The KGB (Soviet political secret police) have taken over the intelligence and espionage services in both Cuba and Nicaragua.

The Soviets have broken the Treaty of Tiatelolco and its Protocol to which it subscribed and ratified, and has ordered its Cuban satellite not to ratify the treaty so Cuba can be used as a Soviet substitute to introduce bombers, submarines and nuclear weapons into Cuba, all in violation of the treaty.

The Soviets and Soviet bloc nations have sent massive shipments of armaments into Nicaragua, including at least 100 T-54 and T-55 tanks, 20 light amphibious tanks, 120 anti-aircraft missiles and more than 700 ground-to-air missiles.

Cuba and Nicaragua serve as bases for the use of offensive weapons by the Soviet Union, whose range covers all of the Caribbean, Central America, Panama, Mexico and most of the United States, posing a definite threat to peace and security in this hemisphere.

In addition to the Soviet-sponsored Cuban terrorist organization known as M-19, there are in Cuba 37 schools for guerrilla indoctrination and training as well as other terrorist training camps. Both Cuba and Nicaragua have introduced into the Americas terrorist groups from the Spanish Basque ETA Separatists, carrying on a communist guerrilla war in northern Spain, and the Arabian Palestinian Liberation Organization, headed by Yassir Arafat who is working hand-in-hand with the Soviets, Castro and Nicaragua. International communist brigades are already operating in several Latin-American countries with a common strategy designed to overthrow the existing governments, especially the new democracies emerging in late 1984 and 1985 as a result of free elections throughout much of South America.

Some of the most damning evidence against Cuba is provided by Cuban exiles themselves. Documents of declarations against Castro's violations of the Monroe Doctrine and also against his violations of human rights in Communist Cuba have been compiled by Dr. Caudio Benedi, the Washington representative of the Junta Patriotica Cubana and by Dr. Benedi and Dr. Manuel A. de Varona, chairman of the same organization. These documents state, in part:

We have denounced before the General Assembly of the Organization of American States that, in violation of all the treaties, agreements, covenants and resolutions in force within the inter-American system, especially the Rio Treaty, the Charter of the Organization of American States, the Monroe Doctrine, the Symms amendment, the Tiatelolco Treaty, and the doctrine and thought of the liberator, Simon Bolivar, the Soviet doctrine of limited sovereignty is presently being applied in Cuba by an extra-continental power, albeit differently as in Czechoslovakia, Poland, and Afghanistan.

In these countries, the Soviet Union sent in its troops and tanks when their peoples declared their will for liberation against the Soviet totalitarian neo-colonialism.

But, in Cuba, the most sophisticated weaponry of the Soviet arsenal has been sent in to prevent an uprising and to maintain the Cuban people and the armed forces simultaneously submitted to the Soviet rule.

The Soviet Union has sent in its troops in a sufficient number to Cuba, disregarding its sovereignty and interfering in the internal affairs of an American state, which is supposedly protected by the treaties, agreements, covenants and resolutions in force within the inter-American system.

It is evident that there is a Soviet combat brigade in Cuba. Besides, we have been able to obtain information from inside Cuba, proving the fact that there are many thousands of Soviet military personnel, of the highest technical and professional ranks, experienced and trained, who, disguised as technicians, diplomats, businessmen, cultural agents, journalists and professors, are actually military personnel, amounting to 25,000.

These military have taken over the political and military direction, as well as the Cuban intelligence, espionage and counter-espionage apparatus.

The Soviet troops are equipped with the most modern and sophisticated weapons of the Soviet arsenal, conveniently located in strategic places. Neither Cuban military personnel, nor the members of the satellite government, are permitted to enter into the location where the most advanced weaponry is kept. Not even their own satellite, Castro, has access to any information concerning these weapons.

The Soviet troops in Cuba have prevented, in all these years, an uprise by the Cuban people against the communist and totalitarian tyranny. The attempts being made, have been suffocated from start, and in the case it would succeed, it would immediately be unmercifully drowned in blood, as was the case with the rebel guerrillas in the Escambray Hills. More than 8,000 Cuban patriots were sacrificed at that time, and 172,000 families in the area of Escambray, were massively displaced, having perpetrated genocide on them. Their houses and all of their belongings were destroyed, and the whole area became a desolated piece of land. The condemned from Condado, a small town near the Escambray, which served as a place of tortures, martydom and suffering to the thousands of Cubans, young and old, men and women, children and ancients. Soviet technicians and Cuban myrmidons, went ahead with the orders coming from Moscow. And the *Cuban holocaust* was silenced. All this, is documented with irrefutable proofs, even by the people who took part in the perpetration and who later deserted; as well as by victims of the said tragedies, and by witnesses with authentic facts.

Any internal uprise of the Cuban people with the Soviet troops in territory of America (Cuba), would also end up drowned in blood.

The Cuban military, many of them tired of serving the Soviet neocolonialism, and hating Communism, cannot organize an uprise against the foreign domination, for several reasons:

1. The Soviet troops dominate the Cuban stage and have better weapons and mobilization facilities.

2. The Cuban troops are not granted the same weapons as the Soviets, and most of the time are disarmed or poorly equipped, to prevent an uprise.

3. The Cuban troops are spread through the national territory, divided in cantons, sections and regions with no communication among them, or coordinated command. They are all subjected to the Soviet central direction.

4. The intelligence and espionage Soviet services inside the Cuban armed forces, direct all the troops, and they have all information regarding everybody's behavior, especially that of the officers.

5. They are constantly indoctrinated about the Soviet superiority and the impossibility of an armed uprise.

Thus, neither the Cuban people, nor the armed forces have been able to carry out, up to the present time, an uprise against the Soviet neocolonialism which would lead to a certain degree of success.

Outside Cuba, the Cuban Exile has been handcuffed by the so-called Kennedy-Kruschev understanding, by which the United States committed themselves, together with the Latin American countries, to prevent the Cuban patriots from preparing a military attack on the Soviet bastion (a subversive military and terrorist base in America). This also explains why the Cuban patriots, in spite of having committed several sporadic heroic acts which have caused many casualties, have not been able to train the Cuban armed forces efficiently, in order to liberate their country.

This has never happened in America; it is an affront and an indignity which affects all the people in this hemisphere, paralyzing and putting in crisis the Inter-Americans System and the Organization of American States Charter.

Not only Cuba is subdued and enslaved. All America is threatened and paralyzed.

The Soviet Union has introduced in Cuba, weapons with which all Latin America and the United States can be attacked successfully.

The Soviet Union uses Cuba and Nicaragua as subversive and terrorist bases against all the Americans which is a violation of the Treaty of Rio; the OAS Charter; The U.N. Charter and the treaties, convenes, agreements and resolutions which are in force in this hemisphere. The Soviet Union has delivered to the Cuban Regime, 240 MIG fighter planes (of the "Foxfire" and "Flogger" types), which are also bombers with a nuclear capability. It has taken to Cuba nuclear submarines (of the "Echo" and Gulf"). We are informed that the Soviet Union keeps deployed in Cuba 6 medium range SS-4 ballistic missiles, out of the 42 it had in Cuba during the so-called "Missile Crisis". It has kept in Cuba several TU-95 "Bear" anti-submarine bombers, as well as recognizing planes. It also maintains strategic-located installations to monitor communications inside the United States and between the U.S. and other Latin American nations.

It has been verified that the Soviet Union has shipped to Cuba an amount of 66,000 tons of military equipment during the last 3 years, over 4 times the amount in stock at the time of the "Missile Crisis". The Soviet Union has built in Cuba a base for nuclear submarines at Cienfuegos Base on the southern coast of Cuba. Nuclear submarines have already been repaired there and there are also wharfs for nuclear weapons and underground locations.

This is why we have told all people in America that, in compliance with all the values and principals of the Inter-American System and the Organization of American States, the Orgainzation of American States Charter, the Rio Treaty, the Monroe Doctrine, the thought and doctrine of the Liberator Simon Bolivar, *it is demanded*, by the means considered pertinent:

1. The departure of the Soviet Combat Brigade of the Territory of the America (Cuba).

2. The departure of all the Soviet military personnel, disguised as diplomats, technicians, businessmen, journalists, cultural agents, etc.

3. The dismantlement of the nuclear submarine base, established by the Soviets in Clenfuegos, Cuba, which has already been utilized in the repair of damaged Soviet submarines.

4. That the Soviets will take out of the Territory of the

America, all offensive weaponry introduced in Cuba.

5. That the so-called Kennedy-Khruschev understanding be declared publicly ineffective.

Thus, the peace and security of America will be guaranteed and Cuban patriots will be able to fight, inside and outside of Cuba, in order to liberate their Country from the Soviet neocolonialism.

Information from trustworthy sources confirm that the Brezhnev doctrine, not only is being applied inside Cuba, but that very soon it is going to be applied in Nicaragua. The Russian troops in Cuba will be carried over there, and gather with the Soviet military, whom, also disguised as diplomats, technicians, businessmen, agricultural advisors, journalists, will be part of the armed forces that will fight the Nicaraguan patriots who struggle for their country's freedom in the fields and in the cities. The Russian troops could eventually fight the American, as well as other Latin American forces, whom, according to the above mentioned treaties, will be forced to carry out a collective action in order to eliminate the Soviet Base from Nicaragua and expel the agents of the Soviet neo-colonialism from this hemisphere.

The memories of the illustrious men of America demand it.

The sovereignty of our peoples demand it.

The effectiveness of the Inter-American System demands it.

The Rio Treaty and the Symms Amendment demand it.

The Organization of American States Charter demands it.

The Tiatelolco Treaty on nuclear arms in Latin America demands it.

The honor and dignity of America demands it.

Either Cuba is saved or America is lost.

Facing up to these threats, it was agreed in the Ninth Consultation Meeting of Foreign Relations Ministers of the Americas that:

"1. The present government of Cuba, since its installation in 1969, has developed and supported and conducted in various manners a policy of intervention in the American Continent, with methods, propaganda, supply of funds, training in sabotage and guerrilla operations, supply of weapons and assistance to movements which tend to the subversion of national institutions through the use of force, in order to install communist regimes."

"2. That support for subversion takes, generally, the form of a political aggression . . ."

"The Ninth Consultation Meeting thus resolves:

"A. To condemn the present government of Cuba as an

aggressor and because of its intervention in the internal affairs of other states, violating their territories and sovereignties."

That judgement and condemnation against the present government of Cuba is in force yet, and since the Ninth Consulation Meeting to date, the government of Cuba has continued to implement the same policy of intervention and violation of sovereignties. The present government of Nicaragua has joined it, because all of that is part and parcel of the expansionist strategy of Soviet neocolonialism into the Americas.

It is incumbent upon you to apply the treaties and covenants which are in force, in order to confront the subversive, terrorist and military aggression in our hemisphere. The "policy of the ostrich", that is, sticking our heads into the sand and carrying on Munich-type negotiations of appeasement, have not rendered any positive results. If we continue to follow that suicidal attitude, the nations of the Americas shall fall, one by one, within the Soviet orbit. If we get together, the Americas will be saved; if we are separated, they will be lost. This was said, with a prophetic foresight, by the illustrious Cuban and American journalist and patriot, Guillermo Martinez Marquez: "Either Cuba is saved or the Americas are lost." Cancer must be eradicated down to its roots and sources. Now there is not only Cuba, but also Nicaragua, and the same will happen to other nations in the Americas, such as Surinam and Guyana, if we do not help them to liberate themselves, as the Caribbean nations and the U.S. helped to liberate Grenada.

The American nations liberated themselves from European colonialism, in the last century through the help of some countries to others. Thus did Simon Bolivar in South-America. Thus was Mexico liberated with the assistance of the United States, and thus was the United States liberated, with the assistance from Cubans, Spaniards, French, Venezuelans, etc. Now, more than ever, the same American patriotic behavior is needed. All for one and one for all. For that purpose, among others, the Inter-American System was established, as well as the OAS, the Rio Treaty, Condeca, the Eastern Caribbean Treaty (OECO), the Treaty of Tiatelolco and rest of the agreements and resolutions in force in the Americas. It is incumbent upon all of us to implement them, before it may be too late.

The goal of the Soviet Union, through its satellites in Cuba and Nicaragua, is to take over all of the American nations. And there cannot be any agreement or compromise regarding that goal. Because of their tactical convenience, they might agree on a "deceitful peace" in Central America, or Colombia, or Peru, or El Salvador, in the same manner that Hitler agreed at Munich; and imitators for Chamberlain will not be lacking in the Americas, ready to let themselves be deceived and to betray the destinies of their nations and the future of the Americas.

Jose Marti, the Apostle of Cuban Independence, said: "To witness a crime in silence is tantamount to commit a crime."

In this American struggle for its freedom and independence, and for the dignity of the American person, "not even the stars can be neutral."

We declare to this honorable general assembly and request from same:

1. That we are entitled to the right to have the voice of the Cuban State heard, "the voice of those who have no voice."

2. That those treaties, covenants, agreements and resolutions in force within the Inter-American System and the OAS, must be enforced.

3. That all Cubans, those inside Cuba and *one million Cubans who are in exile,* are one and make up the democratic Cuban nation, where we have been born and that, together , based upon the experiences of the past, shall build our future with the present as our foundation, without looking back, but only forward.

4. That we reject any kind of coexistence or "detente" negotiation or agreement with the satellite Marxist-Leninist regime of Cuba, the armed instrument and subversive, terrorist and military base of Soviet neocolonialism.

5. That, while we struggle for the independence and liberation of Cuba, we denounce before the Americas and the world the blatant violations of human rights in Cuba, the violations against the American Declaration of Human Rights and Duties and the Universal Declaration of Human Rights, as well as the "cruel, inhuman and degrading treatment that is being endured by Cuban political prisoners, male and female, especially the *"plantados",* who are kept in walled-up cells and the so-called "drawers", subjected to physical and psychological tortures.

6. That freedom is a natural and inalienable right of men and women of all nations, and there cannot be freedom in the Americas while there is no freedom in Cuba, Nicaragua, Suriname and Guyana, submitted to communist totalitarianism.

7. We demand cooperation from all of the American nations, to enforce the Joint Resolution accorded by the United States Congress, known as "Symms Amendment", approved in 1982 and ratified in 1984, which is based upon the Joint Resolutions of 1898 and especially that of 1962, in which the United States obliged itself to struggle jointly with freedom-loving Cubans and

the OAS to attain self-determination for the Cuban people, which is equivalent to freedom and independence for the Cuban people.

8. The Inter-American System, the Organization of American States and each one of the nations and governments of the Americas, have the moral and legal obligation to help the Cuban and Nicaraguan peoples to liberate themselves from the Soviet neocolonialism, maintained there by force and terror, through the Soviet Union's satellite regimes. We Cubans, as well as Nicaraguans, both inside and outside of our respective nations, are in the forefront of the fight, but as in the last century, we need the cooperation of our brother countries in the Americas.

9. That the Soviet Union has announced, upon celebrating the 67th anniversary of the so-called Bolshevik Revolution, that it has made an appeal to intervene in the internal affairs of the Americas, to "liberate" Grenada and consolidate the communist regimes in Nicaragua and Cuba.

10. That the so-called "Kennedy-Krushchev Understanding" always ran counter to the Treaty of Rio, the OAS Charter and those covenants, treaties, agreements and resolutions that are in force in the Americas, and that it has been repeatedly violated by the Soviet Union itself and through the satellite Cuban regime, because of which it is null and void, as President Ronald W. Reagan, of the United States of America, has stated in response to questioning by Cuban journalist Tomas Regalado, Jr. recently, and several Senators have reiterated, such as Steve Symms, John McClure, Jesse Helms and other members of the U.S. Congress, and it has been proven by Cubans.

11. That the Treaty of Rio be enforced regarding the Marxist-Leninist satellite regime of Cuba.

12. That the Marxist-Leninist satellite regime of Nicaragua has mocked the OAS, which in 1979 passed a Resolution that brought about the Sandinistas' access to power, with the obligation to install a pluralistic government with all democratic organizations, to respect human rights and to hold free and democratic elections.

13. That recognition be given us as the representatives of the Cuban State, since the present Cuban regime is excluded from the Inter-American System and the OAS, due to its incompatibility with said system because of its Marxist-Leninist nature.

14. That condemnation be stated against the Institutional Violation of Human Rights in Cuba, in fact and through law, in the light of the American Declaration of Human Rights and Duties and the principles and values of our Judeo-Christian civilization.

15. That the OAS would designate from its midst a decoloniza-

tion committee, to liberate Cuba and Nicaragua from Soviet neo-colonialism.

16. That Cuban political prisoners in American nations, who have been fighting for the liberation of Cuba, be released.

17. That the Soviet Union be forced to withdraw its occupation troops from the territory of an American State (Cuba) and to take away the armaments it has introduced in Cuba, Nicaragua, El Salvador and other American Nations, especially those weapons with a nuclear capability, in violation of the Treaty of Tiatelolco, whose Protocol II it has signed and ratified.

18. That this Fourteenth General Assembly would approve the establishment of a Commissioner for Political Refugees, which problem is already affecting millions of persons in the Americas.

19. That the Cuban and Nicaraguan satellite regimes be cited as participants and culprits in the illegal drug traffic in the Americas.

20. That this General Assembly cite the Cuban and Nicaraguan regimes as aligned and alienated to the Soviet Union.

21. That assistance be given to Cuban, Nicaraguan and Afghan Freedom Fighters, inside and outside of their respective nations.

22. That our belligerence as Freedom Fighters for the liberation of Cuba and Nicaragua be established and recognized, although we shall continue to fight with or without that recognition, as we have been doing thus far.

23. That assistance be given us to dismantle the military, subversive, terrorist, ideological and political bases installed by the Soviet Union in Cuba and Nicaragua, presently used to establish the Soviet neocolonialism in this hemisphere.

24. That Great Britain be forced to negotiate with the Republic of Argentina, and to recognize that the Malvinas are part of Argentina. (Author's note: I personally disagree with this demand.)

25. We salute and support the policies implemented by the President of the United States of America, Ronald W. Reagan, in this hemisphere, stated in his historical speech on February 24, 1982, before the Organization of American States.

26. We support collective action, recognized and in force in the treaties and covenants of the Inter-American System and the OAS, to implement same against the Soviet Union's intervention through its satellites in Cuba, Nicaragua and any other country in the Americas.

27. We state that, had collective action been practiced in Cuba, as it was in the Dominican Republic and Grenada, there would be security, solidarity and peace in the Americas, which shall not

91

exist until all of us, together, shall implement counter-intervention against Soviet Union intervention, and extra-continental interference against which the Liberator Simon Bolivar and the illustrious patriots of the Americas who preceded us, always fought.

28. That this document be circulated among member nations attending this Fourteenth General Assembly meeting of the OAS, since the Cuban state continues to be a member of the Inter-American System and the OAS.

Messrs. Ministers of Foreign Affairs, Ambassadors and Representatives of the American States: We are facing a peculiar historical process, in which none of us is allowed to delegate our responsibilities. History shall judge us all for which we do or fail to do in this fight for freedom and independence in the Americas, for the dignity of American men and women, and for our Judeo-Christian civilization. (End of "Congressional Record" quotes.)

From these resolutions it is obvious that it is not just President Reagan and the anti-communist leaders in the United States who oppose the communist cancer now eating away at the Americas. All the foreign ministers of free Latin American nations oppose communism and jointly seek the help of the United States, both economically and militarily, to defeat communism in this hemisphere.

Evidence that both the Kennedy-Kruschev agreement and the Monroe Doctrine have been violated by communists for 20 years, almost from the moment that the agreement was announced, is revealed by the Central Intelligence Agency. Responding to questions from the Senate Foreign Affairs Committee, the director said:

"The 1962 agreement said the Soviets would send no offensive weapons to Cuba and it also said there would be no export of revolution from Cuba. The agreement has been violated for 20 years."

General David Jones, chairman of the U.S. Joint Chiefs of Staff, appeared as a witness before the House Budget Committee early in 1982 and was asked by Congressman Jack Kemp:

"You talked about the global threat. General Jones, I wanted to ask you, is it not true that those MIG-23 jets on the docks of Cuba, and with the new helicopters in Cuba, and a massive infusion of military equipment by the Soviets in Cuba, that there is a de facto, if not a de jure violation by the Soviet Union of understandings that this country has had with them?"

General Jones answered:

"We interpret it (Soviet actions in Cuba) as a violation. . .In my judgement, they (the Soviets) have gone beyond the 1962 accords and have gone beyond clearly the Monroe Doctrine in Central America. They are now the dominant military power in the Caribbean by a wide, wide margin. They are building up Nicaragua to be the dominant military power in Central America."

The Kennedy-Khruschev agreement has been completely eroded away by Soviet actions in Cuba and the Caribbean. They have done it without so much as trying to hide it and in open, blatant disregard for American public opinion, diplomatic relations, detente, balance of power or any other niceties usually observed between civilized nations concerned with mutual problems.

Comparing Soviet military strength in Cuba in 1962 with today, the buildup is self-evident. At the time of the Kennedy-Khruschev agreement, the Soviets had 75 MIG jet fighters in Cuba and 250 tanks.

Today there are more than 200 Soviet MIGs and some 650 tanks. The number of Soviet MIGs and tanks has tripled in 20 years. Moreover, the Soviets have given the Cuban navy two Foxtrot-style submarines, offensive weapons capable of intercepting U.S. shipping throughout the Caribbean.

This is in direct contravention of the Kennedy-Khruschev Agreement, which says in part:

"Work will cease on offensive missile bases in Cuba and all weapons systems in Cuba capable of offensive use will be rendered inoperable. . .you (Khruschev) agree to remove these weapons systems from Cuba under appropriate United Nations supervision and undertake to halt the further introduction of such weapons into Cuba. . .Khruschev stated that we (the Soviets) have instructed our officers to take the necessary measures to stop the construction of the facilities indicated — missile sites — and to dismantle and return them to the Soviet Union. I consider my letter to you as firm understandings on the part of our governments which should be promptly carried out."

The United States foreign policy in regard to powers outside the Western Hemisphere, establishing themselves or any part of their political systems in this part of the world, dates not only to the Monroe Doctrine of 1823 but has been implemented in many subsequent treaties and policies such as the Rio Treaty of 1947, the 1954 Act of Bogota, the Costa Rica Communique of 1960 and the Punta Del Este Communique of 1961.

The heart, meaning and intent of the Monroe Doctrine was included in a message President Monroe sent to Congress in 1823. It was a time when, much like today, European powers were attempting to re-extend their dominion over the new independent nations of Latin America which had just won their freedom from Spain and Portugal. Before he made the message to Congress public, Monroe conferred with past Presidents James Madison and Thomas Jefferson, and with his own secretary of State and future president, John Quincy Adams, who drafted the document. So the doctrine was not merely a whim or passing thought of Monroe. Modern critics have claimed it was designed with imperialistic motives by the United States but there is absolutely nothing in the writings and papers of Monroe, Madison, Jefferson and Adams to indicate that any of these men had anything but the highest humanitarian motives in mind when they agreed on Monroe's policy. The doctrine certainly must be credited with the continued independence of the South American Republics. It's most important part said:

"We owe it, therefore, to candor and to the amicable relations existing between the United States and those powers to declare that we should consider any attempt on their part to extend their system to any portion of this hemisphere as dangerous to our peace and safety. . .it is impossible that the allied powers should extend their political system to any portion of either continent without endangering our peace and happiness."

In an international agreement designed to secure world peace in the years following World War I, the Monroe Doctrine was mentioned specifically as a foregone conclusion of U.S. foreign policy:

"The United States regards the Monroe Doctrine as a part of its national security and defense. Under the right of self-defense allowed by the treaty must necessarily be included the right to maintain the Monroe Doctrine which is part of our system of national defense. . ."

As trouble with Spain was brewing over the issue of Cuban independence in the 1890s, President Grover Cleveland cited the Monroe Doctrine, saying:

"The doctrine upon which we stand is strong and sound because its enforcement is important to our peace and safety as a nation, and is essential to the integrity of our free institutions and the tranquil maintenance of our distinct form of government."

As World War I loomed on the horizon in the summer of 1914, U.S. Secretary of State Elihu Root interpreted the Monroe Doctrine for the foreign powers about to involve themselves in the conflict, saying:

"The Monroe Doctrine is not international law, but it rests

upon the right of self-protection and that right is recognized by international law. The right is a necessary corollary of independent sovereignty. It is well understood that the exercise of the right of self-protection may, and frequently does, extend in its effect beyond the limits of the territorial jurisdiction of the State exercising it. . .Since the Monroe Doctrine is a declaration based upon this nation's right to self-protection, it cannot be transmuted into a joint, or common, declaration by American States, or any number of them. It is to be observed that in reference to the South American governments, as in all other respects, the international right upon which the declaration expressly rests is not sentiment or sympathy or a claim to dictate what kind of government any other country shall have, but the safety of the United States. It is because the new governments cannot be overthrown by the allied powers 'without endangering our peace and happiness' that 'the United States cannot behold such interposition with indifference.'"

There was no doubt in the minds of American leaders for more than a century, of the fact that the Monroe Doctrine is an expression of our inherent right to self-defense and there should be no doubt about it today. Those who speak against resisting communist aggression in El Salvador or Central America or South America are ignoring the intent of the Monroe Doctrine which considers the security of this hemisphere vital to our national security. It is not only a matter of permitting El Salvador to settle its own difficulties with the communists, it also is a matter of American national security under the Monroe Doctrine. It is only since the end of World War II that weak and frightened voices in Washington have urged abandonment of the Monroe Doctrine.

President Kennedy obviously had the Monroe Doctrine in mind during his inaugural address on January 20, 1962, when he said:

"Let every nation know, whether it wishes us well or ill, that we shall pay any price, bear any burden, meet any hardships, support any friends, oppose any foe, in order to assure the survival and the success of liberty. This much we pledge and more."

And Kennedy was virtually prophetic in 1962 as the Cuban missile crisis was building when he said:

"We face a relentless struggle in every corner of the globe that goes far beyond the clash of armies or even nuclear armaments. The armies are there, and in large number. The nuclear armaments are there. But they serve primarily as the shield behind which subversion, infiltration, and a host of other tactics steadily advance, picking off vulnerable areas one by one in situations which do not permit our own armed intervention. . .Our security may be lost piece by piece, country by country, without the firing of a single missile or the crossing of a single border."

And during the missile crisis later in 1962, Kennedy said:

"If at any time the communist buildup in Cuba were to endanger or interfere with our security in any way, including our base at Guantanamo, our passage to the Panama Canal, our missile and space activities at Cape Canaveral, or the lives of American citizens in this country, or if Cuba should ever attempt to export its aggressive purposes by force, or the threat of force, against any nation in this hemisphere, or become an offensive military base of significant capacity for the Soviet Union, then this country will do whatever must be done to protect its own security and that of its allies."

Looking back at the significance and the greatness of the Monroe Doctrine and the words of American statesmen who have explained it and interpreted again and again down through the years to our enemies and to our friends, America is faced today with the decision of whether we are at last to truly abandon this remarkable keystone of foreign policy in this hemisphere. The case is made so clearly that the Monroe Doctrine is based on the principle of international law and that law being that every nation has a right to self-defense. Communist military aggression in Latin America jeopardizes the security of the United States if it goes unchallenged and a domino theory becomes a reality on the mainland of the Americas in Latin America.

We simply cannot overlook what the Cuba of Fidel Castro is doing today. Cuba has troops in more than a dozen African countries and in Nicaragua. There is overwhelming evidence that Cuba has been supporting the communist guerrillas in El Salvador. There can be no question that this is a definite threat to our own security.

And what of Cuba's master, its string-puller and bankroller? We need only ask the people of Afghanistan or Poland or Czechoslovakia or Hungary how they are doing under communist rule directed from Moscow. The Soviets have been taking one country after another, proving the domino theory is a reality.

We need only ask the "Boat People" of Southeast Asia where we were betrayed by our own Congress into losing the Vietnam War about how things are going with communism, or ask the survivors of the genocide victims in Laos and Cambodia. People say we don't want another Vietnam in El Salvador, but what if we get it anyway whether we want it or not or even fight there or not? God help America if El Salvador falls! We will witness a trek of refugees and immigrants fleeing from communism — "voting with their feet" — unprecedented in the Western Hemisphere. It will begin in El Salvador and as the dominoes fall it will extend through the rest of Central America and Mexico and there will be millions of people walking across the 2,100-mile border of the United States and Mexico in an immigration into this country of unimaginable proportions!

The refugees will come first, just ahead of the communist guerillas and regulars. What will we do then? Try to turn them back at the border, at the Rio Grande? We can't even do that now as the flood of illegal Mexican aliens continues to pour into this country in ever-increasing numbers each year. How would we hold back entire hordes and populations marching relentlessly into the United States, much in the manner the Cubans poured out of Cuba into Florida when given the chance in 1981? Are we going to shoot them all? Are we going to just give up to them and let them overrun the country?

If we don't want to face such a decision in the near future, the time to solve the problem is now, by invoking the Monroe Doctrine against communist aggression in Latin America and once again against the Soviet Union in Cuba as well as against Fidel Castro's regime busy exporting revolution everywhere it can.

America must reaffirm the Monroe Doctrine with new vigor, calling for U.S. resistance to Cuban aggression and subversion in this hemisphere, prevention of the escalation and proliferation of Soviet bases and Soviet influence in Cuba, and strong support for the fundamental principle of self-determination for the Cuban people.

America must let the Soviets and Cuba and the whole world know exactly where we stand, if we stand anywhere, and exactly what we stand for, if we still stand for anything.

Our news media, instead of taking such delight in destroying first one and then another of our American presidents, should be telling Americans and the world in a loud, clear and unmistakable voice about the Cuban troops that went to Angola with Soviet weapons and took that country for communism. They should tell about the communists in Mozambique, in Rhodesia (now Zimbabwe), and about the 26,000 Cuban troops in starving Ethiopia. They should publish and broadcast the details of the Cuban-organized "international brigade" that fought in Nicaragua and helped turn it into a communist country and now is providing leadership for communist revolution in El Salvador.

Instead we have a Congress that nips and nibbles at the administration of the first strong anti-communist president we have had in years, aided by a news media more interested in tearing down the White House than in opposing communism right in our own backyard. We have a Congress that hesitates and fools around and debates endlessly and takes so much time making decisions, if any, about communist aggression that the world does not know where we stand or for what we stand. This weak and cowardly and evasive national attitude toward communism as reflected by Congress only encourages the communists to further boldness, aggression and conquest.

What President Reagan has said about taking a stand on the national economy and getting this country back in some kind of respectable financial shape again should go for our opposition to communism, too: If not us, who? If not now, when?

The Soviet Union, thousands and thousands of miles away, should not be involved in any sort of substantial political or military role in the Caribbean or Central America or South America.

We talk about winning the battle for men's minds in our struggle with communism. In Cuba, or the Isle of Pines, now called the Isle of Youth, there are 60 senior high school complexes, many of which are given over to educating students from a particular foreign country in which the Soviet Union and Cuba have an interest. In one of these high schools, there are 600 Namibian students enrolled. Namibia used to be called Southwest Africa and has been governed by the Republic of South Africa since World War I. In recent years, communist guerrillas have been attacking Namibia and the communist-bloc in the United Nations has demanded "self-. determination" and "liberation" for it.

Many of the brightest of the 600 high school students from Namibia getting an education courtesy of the Soviet Union and Cuba will go on to universities in Russia, such as Patrice Lummumba University in Moscow, for advanced education. In the Cuban high schools they are taught Marxism and Leninism in classrooms decorated with the portraits of those two great masters of evil and bedecked with communist sloganeering. These students will, in the future, be the leaders of Namibia, the statesmen, lawyers, doctors, engineers, teachers, journalists, government officials.

In the United States, according to State Department information about education exchange students, we presently are educating two students from Namibia. Two compared with 600 in Cuba!

Here as much as anyplace is where a great danger lies for the future. We are losing the battle with communism for men's minds. We are losing the propaganda battle with communism. We are losing the military battle with communism This battle is on our doorstep in Cuba and in our backyard in Central America. It is directed from Moscow through Havana but it is right upon us and time is running out.

In case anyone has forgotten, America stands for freedom and democracy. The Soviet Union's invasion of Afghanistan and Cuba's aggression in Africa and Latin America shows that they stand for terror, repression and conquest. Contrary to the Monroe Doctrine, we are allowing a foreign influence from far outside this hemisphere to exert its influence over our neighbors. The Kremlin gets a bargain basement price in its support of Castro's Cuba, $3 billion to $4 billion annually, about what the General Accounting Office estimates is lost in waste, fraud and abuse each year within the U.S. Department of Health and Human Resources. For this price, the Soviet-Cuban Axis has 50,000 Soviet-trained and Soviet-armed Cuban troops serving in a dozen countries while 100,000 Soviet troops try to bring Afghanistan to heel.

The Soviets broke the Kennedy-Khrushchev Agreement while we kept it. We agreed to undertake no action against the Castro regime as the price for withdrawal of Soviet missiles from Cuba. Now the missiles are back along with troops, ships, planes. . .the whole military apparatus. But we still honor the broken agreement while the Soviets would have us enter yet others on disarmament, nuclear weapons and the like. We never seem to learn that you can't trust the communists.

By breaking the Kennedy-Khrushchev Agreement and ignoring the Monroe Doctrine, the Soviet Union assured itself of a continuing base of operations 90 miles off our coast. And by using Cuba and Cuban troops to press its revolutionary goals, the Soviet Union has neatly side-stepped any semblance of heavy-handed aggression that so concerns Third World nations, with the exception of remote Afghanistan.

The success of this Soviet-Cuban connection simply shows the gullibility and even hypocrisy of many Third World nations and also many Americans. Castro poses as a "non-aligned" leader to shield his aggression. The majority of members in the United Nations General Assembly proclaim Cuban troops in Africa as "volunteers" in defense of freedom and democracy. Andrew Young, our former U.N. ambassador, called the Cubans a force for "stability" in Africa. The U.N. General Assembly Third Worlders call the Soviet Union a peace-loving friend while condemning the United States and Israel as imperialist aggressors. Many within our own State Department agree.

The irony of the Soviet-Cuban violation of the Monroe Doctrine and the Kennedy-Khrushchev Agreement is that it was forged from the failure of communism itself. Castro replaced Batista's government with something far worse, a communism featuring political repression, torture, murder and severe economic privation.

Only a massive transfusion of rubles and rifles have kept Cuba from total collapse. The Soviets subsidize Cuba at a cost of $8 million to $12 million a day on the island where the socialist dream of more than 20 years ago has become the economic nightmare of today.

The fact is, as Cuba shows so clearly, communist revolutions and socialist states do not produce the propaganda book picture of oppressed masses emerging arm-in-arm into a new era of economic progress, social equality and political freedom. Instead, communism offers only harsher and more brutal standards than any it might replace. Communism exercises almost total control, practically eliminating any possibility of a counter-revolution or a free election. Without outside intervention, a communist revolution is virtually irreversible.

Yet the news media and leftist politicians and educators and clergy and other "liberal" spokesmen continue to delude themselves and their listeners with totally untrue romanticized versions of left-wing revolutionaries while denouncing what they consider right-wing dictatorships no matter what the state of comparable economics or freedoms.

In the face of all this evidence, American policy makers, news media, intellectuals and the people themselves can't seem to choose between even the lesser of two evils in Latin America. Rather than invoke the Monroe Doctrine with all dispatch and strength, we continue to listen to the siren song of revolution and its completely unreal "romance." Such things as "agrarian reform" seem so enticing when reality shows it is not reform at all but seizure of land by the state. Any redistribution of it to "peasants" is only a limited basis for propaganda purposes and even that is kept under strict control. Red China has had almost 40 years to implement its promised "agrarian reform" and hasn't done so yet. Soviet Russia has had about 70 years. Castro has had more than 25 years. But in El Salvador the Carter administration forced a land collectivization scheme on that country between 1977 and 1979, which set off the reaction that led to civil war and communist revolution-invasion. Carter also wound up supporting the communist Sandinistas in Nicaragua and the communist Manley regime in Jamaica.

Such a policy is madness. It is clear beyond reasonable doubt that Castro's Cuba is a communist state operated on behalf of the Soviet Union. Without armed intervention there seems no way to reverse the communist revolution there. If the Cuban people must endure the political repression and economic deprivation forced upon them by the Castro regime because they are too weak to throw off its yoke, Washington wants only to sympathize with them at this time.

But when Castro's Cuba trys to export that misery to other Latin American nations with the help of the Soviet Union, it becomes the business of the United States under the obligations of the Monroe Doctrine and the Kennedy-Khrushchev Agreement that we still honor them even if the Soviets don't, to say "No! Enough! Stop where you are!"

If we don't, they are not going to stop even when they reach the Rio Grande. Then the tramping feet of the army of refugees coming across our border will finally bury our long-ignored and seemingly powerless Monroe Doctrine.

Chapter 5

NOW THE INVASION:
AMERICA AT BAY!

Communism is on the march in Central America and the Caribbean, armed, confident, and with the indirect support of the U.S. Congress in many ways.

In all the countries ringing the Caribbean, communist power is seen in its armed might, revolutionary violence, political influence and the news media manipulation. From Panama through Central America and Mexico, over to Cuba and back through the Caribbean Islands, the force of communism has broken the Monroe Doctrine, shattered all American foreign policy planning the region from Roosevelt's Good Neighbor Policy to Reagan's Caribbean Initiative.

The forces of freedom are in confused retreat nearly everywhere in the region except in El Salvador where the communist revolution is being opposed militarily but the vital American economic and military aid is constantly imperiled by U.S. Congressional liberals who seem to be in sympathy with the communists. Here is a brief country-by-country rundown of what's happening in this area of top priority so vital to the security interests of the United States:

PANAMA—The Panama Canal was given away in 1979 by President Jimmy Carter and liberal senators, to the late communist dictator Omar Torrijos. After the giveaway, sensational testimony before a Senate Subcommittee, testimony ignored or suppressed by the major national news media, revealed that major multi-national banks and international financial interests pressured Carter to give away the canal so Panama could use canal tolls to pay off its $2 billion debt to the United Nations International Monetary Fund and World Bank. Canal tolls won't go to boost the Panama economy as Carter had said but will, instead, be funneled into the one-world international monetary system controlled by major international bankers.

COSTA RICA—This small democratic and prosperous nation has no army and only a small national police force equipped to enforce civil law, not fight military battles. Sandwiched between communist Panama and communist Nicaragua, Costa Rica can be taken at leisure by the communists when they are ready. Costa Rica is under great pressure from international communism for allowing anti-communist exiles from Nicaragua such as the famed Commander Zero and other "contras" (meaning counter revolutionaries against communism, or freedom fighters) safe haven in Costa Rica. How much longer Costa Rica can take the pressure is debatable without substantial help from the United States.

NICARAGUA—America's only reliable ally in the area, Anastasio Somoza, was overthrown by communist revolutionaries in 1979 when Carter withdrew aid from Somoza who fled to exile and was later assassinated by communist gunmen. Since then Nicaragua has been the mainland funnel for Soviet and Cuban military assistance to communist revolutionaries attempting to seize the government of neighboring El Salvador by force. President Reagan has revealed previously secret intelligence photos of 31 Soviet-built military bases in Nicaragua. Congress still cut back his request for increased military aid to El Salvador. Nicaragua has been engaged in border warfare with another neighbor, Honduras. Thousands of Soviet and Cuban advisers and dozens of Soviet tanks and warplanes are stationed at the new Nicaraguan military bases. Meanwhile, Nicaragua oppresses its own people and has carried on a deliberate policy of genocide and relocation of native Meskito Indians and other Indian tribes being forced off their time-honored land occupancy in northeast Nicaragua and in other remote areas of the country.

HONDURAS—Honduras is probably the next communist target in Central America should El Salvador fall. Nervous but determined Honduras officials have given exile to many Nicaraguans who fled the communist takeover. They have now organized into counter-revolutionary forces and have been harrassing the communist flank along the Honduras-Nicaragua border, taking some pressure off El Salvador. U.S. aid to the "contras" has drawn fire from liberals in Congress who consider it illegal for the United States to help anyone take their country back once it has fallen to communism.

EL SALVADOR—Scene of the most vicious fighting in Central America since Nicaragua fell. In 1982 the people elected a fairly strong, conservative government and reaffirmed it in 1985 elections. Communists refused to participate in the elections except to try to disrupt polling places with violence. It didn't work. Most Salvadorans declare by their votes and actions that they don't want to live under communism and they are willing to resist it. They are much further advanced economically, spiritually and militarily than was the government of South Vietnam. They say their country will not become "another Vietnam" as many American liberals argue.

GUATEMALA—This country is one big cotton field, almost impossible to defend. It has been used as an arsenal by communists at times for storage of weapons awaiting transshipment to communist guerrillas in neighboring El Salvador. The Guatemalan government is anti-communist but is too weak militarily to defend itself without American help.

BELIZE—Formerly the British colony of British Honduras, the recently independent government is considered incapable of resisting either communist revolution from within or invasion from across its border with Guatemala and Mexico or from the sea. Some retired British military men serve as advisers to the woefully inadequate security forces only slowly being beefed up as the fighting in Central America continues.

MEXICO—The communist controlled government of Mexico has been paying blackmail to both Nicaragua and Cuba to forestall a new Mexican communist revolution. President de la Madrid claims to be non-communist but is surrounded in the gigantic and corrupt Mexican bureaucracy and state government by known communists in key positions, including the governor of one Mexican state bordering the United States. The "blackmail" has been in the form of some $70 million in "foreign aid" to Cuba and Nicaragua at the cost of a drastically deflated peso and acceptance of massive injections of funds from the International Monetary Fund. Many see considerable irony in Mexico helping to finance communist revolution in the region while American taxpayers support Mexico and the IMF through United Nations contributions by the U.S. and by money manipulation by the Federal Reserve System.

CUBA—Cuba has never been stronger militarily. Massive Soviet military aid to help the communist revolutionaries in Nicaragua and El Salvador are funneled through Cuba, which takes what it wants first from the Red supply pipeline. Thousands of Soviet military advisers, soldiers, sailors, civil workers and bureaucrats are in Cuba — while thousands of Cuban soldiers do Russia's dirty work in Africa. Fidel Castro is as anti-American as ever and the Cuban people suffer as they always have since Castro came to power in 1959. The Soviets have 14 major military bases in Cuba.

HAITI—Located just off the east coast of Cuba, this bankrupt nation sharing part of an island with the Dominican Republic is too poor for even the communists to want very much. Haitian refugees from some of the worst poverty in the Western Hemisphere continue to risk their lives as "boat people" to reach Florida. Many die. Haiti has been in the news recently as a source of the homosexual diseases Herpes and AIDS because many New York City "gays" have vacationed there in recent years for the cheap sex available.

DOMINICAN REPUBLIC—Only American armed intervention in the Dominican Republic in 1965 saved this weak island nation from a communist revolution. Now the communists are at it again with increased efforts fostered by Castro to unite communist party factions on the island and prepare them for revolution. Many Dominican "students" are being trained in Havana and Moscow.

PUERTO RICO—Off the east coast of Haiti-Dominican Republic, this U.S. territory is frequently in turmoil over phony demands for "independence" by a small but vocal communist organization which believes an independent government could be easily overthrown, knowing the U.S. won't let the communists seize Puerto Rico as long as it is a U.S. territory. Considered to be safely under U.S. protection despite periodic violence and assassinations.

JAMAICA—South of Cuba, Jamaica has made great economic strides since the 1980 election which ousted the Marxist Michel Manley after eight years of misrule and mismanagement. Inflation is down from 25 to 1.2 per cent, crime is down 39 per cent, the black market has been nearly eliminated and foreign investment is on the rise. The free election of Edgar Seaga, a Kingston lawyer, changed everything for the better in Jamaica and it stands in shining contrast to the communist violence and ruination going on around it in the Caribbean region.

GRENADA—Freed from communist domination by President Reagan's daring military liberation stroke, Grenada has since held free elections to install a democratic government and has taken to free enterprise. Grenada is a shining example of what American military might can accomplish in the Latin American region when the press does not appoint itself as arbitrary critic and defeatist general and when Congressional liberals can interfere only afterwards.

GUYANA—The scene of the infamous James Jones suicide-massacre, this South American mainland nation sharing a border with Venezuela has gone completely communist. The Soviets have built 10 military bases there. It should be recalled that Jones, the phony "evangelist" who led a colony of blacks from San Francisco to their suicide deaths in Guyana, was a communist who had bilked thousands of their savings over the years and turned much of the money over to the Soviet embassy in Guyana. The country lives on a backward agriculture and cattle economy along with Soviet expenditures made there in connection with the military bases construction and maintenance.

SOUTH AMERICA—It is obvious that communist conquest of Central America and the major Caribbean Islands would cut the lifeline between North America and South America. Nearly all South American countries have strong communist party organizations in comparison with North America. Many of them are training and waiting for communist success in Central America as a signal for them to rise against the governments of South American nations, expecting communist forces in the Caribbean region to keep the U.S. too busy to rescue its South American friends who have been installing freely-elected governments.

SUMMARY—Red power has expanded rapidly in Central America and the Caribbean region. El Salvador is still probably the key to the future of the area. If it falls to the communists there is little hope the rest can be saved. Mexico is rotten from its inside corrupt government core out to its thin worthless peso skin. It is a sick nation that major oil discoveries have been unable to cure. It will fall like an overripe plum when the communists want it, and so will most of the island countries if El Salvador goes down and America retreats from this vital region. The battle line will then shift to the Rio Grande and the borders of Texas, New Mexico, Arizona and Southern California. By then South America would be in the throes of communist revolution if not already conquered. The U.S. could expect no help from there and they would be beyond help from the U.S.

Chapter 6

MEXICO'S COMMUNIST CURSE

Mexico is a communist nation in all but name. It is owned, operated and controlled by a "Communist Mafia" consisting of Red bureaucrats who dictate the government and its policies. The president of Mexico is only a public relations figurehead.

Manuel Moreno Rivas, an expert in Latin American political affairs, says this about Mexico:

"The communists have taken an active and important part in every significant issue of Mexican politics since 1918."

And President Reagan says this: "I am deeply concerned about the safety of Americans in Mexico."

There is no "reform" in Mexico. Its major exports to the United States are illegal aliens and drugs. The communists running Mexico have planned it that way.

Communist-controlled Mexico has become an enemy of the United States and is pursuing a policy designed to drive millions of Mexicans into the U.S., to terrorize and intimidate Americans in Mexico and to reclaim vast areas of the southwestern United States as a part of a communist revolution.

The American news media has been ignoring this direct threat to the security of the United States too long. Only the kidnapping and murder of an American Drug Enforcement Agency official in Guadalajara — practically on the doorstep of the U.S. Consulate Office there — finally prompted the major national news media to become concerned with events in Mexico. Even now, they can't bring themselves to blame communists for the trouble.

A customs crackdown at the U.S.-Mexican border that inconvenienced thousands of travelers as U.S. agents searched for clues to the crime attracted considerable press attention but no in-depth study of the communist control of Mexico.

Another major clue to communism's grip on Mexico was when the Mexican "government", such as it is, controlled by communist bureaucrats, turned down construction of a new IBM plant because IBM would not surrender 51 per cent control to Mexico. The communists in the Mexican government who decide such issues demand 51 per cent control of all foreign business enterprises stationed in Mexico.

This policy is consistent with the seizure by the "Communist Mafia" which has run Mexico's major industries for years and most of the land.

The Mexican government now owns 78 per cent of all the land in Mexico, having begun to seize it in 1934. It seized the Mexican petroleum industry and "nationalized" American petroleum interests and investments there in 1938. Today, the communist-controlled Mexican government owns the railroads, the airlines and aviation companies, the electric power, the one and only telephone company, the fishing industry, the main mining works, the sugar factories, the iron and steel foundaries, the oil wells and gasoline refineries, the petrochemical industry and many other vital operations upon which Mexico and virtually all Mexicans are dependent, including the banks.

The communists in Mexico are today and have been for years dedicated to the destruction of private enterprise.

Communist Mafia

The Communist Mafia of Mexican bureaucrats have 392 agencies, branches, offices and delegations — known as the "Empresas para-esta-tales" or state enterprises — which constitute the machinery of the government for state control of every single yield of Mexican farming, fishing, mining, energy production, commerce, transportation and finance.

There are thousands of Soviet agents infiltrated into every political organization and movement in Mexico, receiving orders issued from the Kremlin and passed on by the Soviet embassy in Mexico City. Using Mexican native communists, many of whom have been trained and indoctrinated in the Soviet Union, the Soviets take advantage of every point of strife, discussion or struggle in Mexico to present communism as the medicine that will cure all evils.

Within the communist organization in Mexico are found

most high ranking government officials, financiers, college professors, intellectuals, writers, artists and heads of industry who know, collectively, to perfection how to bring about, with official help, economic movements and crisis that will produce poverty and hunger so that the communists may appear as the redeemers and make the communist banner looked upon as the only solution to all important problems.

This Communist Mafia has deliberately imposed upon Mexico a poverty that serves two purposes: (1) to drive millions of poverty-stricken Mexicans into the United States where they can later be called upon to rise up in communist-inspired revolution, and (2) to make life so hard for the rest of the millions of Mexicans that they will join the communists as a last resort for survival.

As soon as the communists took control of Russia in 1917, they turned their attention to Mexico, where in 1918 there was still a bloody revolution going on that was destroying the country, a time when nobody paid any attention to the infiltration of thousands of communist agents. Trotsky fled Lenin's brand of communism to seek refuge in Mexico only to be assassinated by Soviet agents there.

The communists in Mexico have received an excellent education, specializing in the knowledge and language of Mexico, its history, its social and economic situation, the psychology of Mexicans and how they react to different incentives and pressures.

They have, over the years, established personal dossiers on every important or potentially important Mexican and developed in each individual case a policy on how to handle them, playing upon their known weaknesses, undermining their strengths, manipulating events around them, blackmailing them to turn into communists as the price they must pay to achieve high office, importance or success in their chosen fields.

Reds Supervise Education

Since the 1930s, the communists targeted education as the most effective weapon to attain their goals in Mexico and have controlled the Secretaria de Education Publica, the equivalent of our federal education department. Teachers are routinely trained by communist education officials.

For generations, the children of Mexico have been taught to hate the "imperialist Americans" and to worship communist heroes. In the free government textbooks of Mexico, precious little is said about non-communist Mexican heroes of the past

111

but there is an abundance of material about Marx, Lenin, Stalin, Mao, Castro and the alleged "martyrdom" of Che Guevara, assassinated — according to Mexican textbooks — by American agents.

Most of the teachers in Mexico are members of the Communist Party. Their jobs are virtually dependent upon it. The late Augustin Reyes Heroles, who died in 1985, ruled Mexican education with an iron hand and many dedicated communists within his department have been trained as his successor. He was an openly-avowed communist militant considered as one of the heads of the Red international staff. He had previously been Secretary of the Interior, ruling the Mexican petroleum industry and land policy. His move to education was an indication of how important the Soviets consider education control in Mexico to be. They are not about to relinquish it simply because Reyes Heroles died.

The Mexican president is a joke. He claims to be a non-communist (but not an anti-communist) but in fact he is mothing but a front man for the Communist Party in Mexico to fool the American news media and public into thinking that Mexico is not controlled by communists.

Red Corruption's Legacy

Eliminating communist corruption in Mexico would be like eliminating ice in the Artic. Corruption is why Mexico is a debtor nation despite its long-time oil wealth. Consider this:

In 1970, at the end of the term of President Gustavo Diaz Ordaz, the external debt of Mexico was $3.6 billion. During the following 12 years, under Presidents Luis Echeverria, another avowed communist, and his hand-picked successor, Jose Lopez Portillo, Mexico's national debt has increased to $80 billion!

During that same period, a total of $70 billion in oil revenues became available to the Echeverria and Portillo administrations. The $70 billion plus the $80 billion in-flow of borrowed foreign money (mostly American) totals $150 billion. What has the government of Mexico done with $150 billion in foreign capital sent into the country as payments for oil and as loans? How was it possible that big international bankers failed to notice the disappearance of that much money until just recently?

If it had been truly invested in Mexico, that country would have been transformed into the most developed country in Latin America. Instead, the Mexican peso has become virtually worthless, the country is for all accounts and pur-

poses bankrupt, and Mexico is in the worst crisis of its history.

The answer is that the Communist Mafia that controls the Mexican government has stolen the billions and put the money to its own uses.

Here is what the communists have done to Mexico:

• Decreased the value of the peso from 12.50 per dollar to what is now a "free market" rate of less than one cent per peso.

• This tremendous devaluation has made it at least five times as hard for Mexico to repay its international debts.

• The Bank of Mexico has been seized by "the government" and its control over the current rate of exchange has led to the expropriation and nationalization of private banks.

• The communist-controlled United Nations and its International Monetary Fund — financed largely by the United States — has imposed an "austerity" program on Mexico in order to be sure the debts will be repaid. This "austerity" program comes out of the hide of the long-suffering Mexican people, forcing them further into poverty and hoplessness.

The $150 billion stolen by the communists could have helped solve or at least alleviate some of the following problems that plague Mexico City, the supposed "pride" or "crown jewel" of Mexico:

1. Two million people in Mexico City have no running water. For most, an entire block share one water faucet. Any day in Mexico City and many other Mexican towns and villages, a visitor can see long lines of people with jars and jugs and buckets standing in line for hours each morning for their daily water supply from one faucet serving hundreds to thousands of people.

2. Three million people in Mexico City have no sanitary sewage facilities so tons of human waste are left in gutters or vacant lots to dry and eventually contaminate the dust that chokes millions of city residents, causing untold numbers of lung and bronchial ailments.

3. Millions of rats roam the city because of 14,000 tons of daily garbage, only about 8,000 tons gets picked up or processed. Some is dumped in landfills but most is left to rot in the open.

4. There is no air pollution control and the city is permanently enveloped in a brown haze of polluted air that during rush hour limits vision to a couple of blocks or less. The chemical air pollutants amount to 11,000 tons daily and breathing it is equivalent to each person in Mexico City smoking two packs of cigarettes a day.

5. Chemical and biological poisoning kills 30,000 children

every year through respiratory and gastrointestinal diseases. Another 70,000 adults are estimated to die annually from similar ailments.

This is the legacy of communism, and its corruption and theft.

There is no reasonable possibility that Mexico will ever cleanse itself of the communist poison now polluting it. The United States has been trying by diplomatic and economic means to "do something" for Mexico for years without any tangible positive results but with appalling examples of negative results.

Today, big American banks and middle-management State Department personnel are in charge of American policy toward Mexico. This style of "negotiations" with Mexico have done nothing but reinforce communism and its socialist characteristics there.

These liberal bankers (persuading Congress to pump U.S. taxpayer dollars into the U.N.'s International Monetary Fund for Mexico) and the liberal diplomats of the State Department (working hand-in-hand with the Mexican communists) have created a revolutionary problem south of the border of incalcuable seriousness. They have, in effect, become allied with the Communist Mafia controlling Mexico.

The weakness of American resolve to stop communism in Nicaragua and other nations of Central America (President Reagan has to fight Congress for every dollar to help anti-communist nations and movements there) has encouraged the Mexican communists.

The free world has in recent times lost China, Cuba, Vietnam, Cambodia, big parts of Africa, much of Afghanistan and all of Nicaragua to communism. There is an immediate risk that communism is going to spread over Central America because a cowardly Congress — just as it did in Vietnam — refuses to support anti-communism

Mexico is communist controlled, whether we like it or not. The press still clings to the false belief that Mexican President de la Madrid can somehow "save" the country with his already discredited and abandoned "reform" program while refusing to investigate or publish the truth about the Communist Mafia.

We have no illusions about the communist control of Mexico and refuse to fall for the clap-trap emanating from Washington about any cordial U.S.-Mexico relations.

Beware of Mexican "Bargains"

President Reagan has recognized the danger of Mexico to U.S. citizens there and is aware that in addition to the much-publicized kidnapping of the U.S. drug agent that there have been many mysterious disappearances of Americans and several assaults, including a murder and rape of U.S. citizens.

Americans seeking Mexican tourist "bargains" because of the low peso evaluation had best consider the risks and dangers facing any "gringos" going to Mexico today. Every American tourist is under some degree of communist surveillance in Mexico.

And the United States itself is under Kremlin-directed Mexican Communist Mafia surveillance which constantly evaluates when the proper time might be for export of communist revolution into the Southwest of the U.S. Every Mexican school child for the last three generations have been taught that California and the Southwestern states of Arizona, New Mexico, Texas and parts of Colorado and Utah "rightfully" belong to Mexico and it is Mexico's eventual "destiny" to reclaim them someday.

The Kremlin-directed infiltration of illegal Mexican aliens into the United States (on a much larger scale than Castro's Cuban infiltration) is only a forerunner, a foundation-layer, of the planned communist invasion of America from south of the Rio Grande.

Since the devaluations of the peso in Mexico, the tide of illegal Mexican aliens sneaking into the United States has risen to alarming heights. They are not only taking jobs away from America's unemployed, many of them are communist-trained revolutionaries being planted here now for a future uprising.

And it is not just Mexican aliens swamping the U.S. The Environmental Fund study of immigration reports that an alien enters the United States every minute on the average and that primarily because of alien immigration, both legal and illegal, the population of the United States is now around 240 million, or maybe 250 counting illegal aliens, will reach 303 million by the year 2000. Immigration now constitutes about half the population growth in the United States and is expected to grow even more.

There are 200 million people in Latin America ready to immigrate and 95 per cent of them want to come to the United States. And that doesn't include aliens from Asia and elsewhere.

Ten Million Illegally Working Now!

The Environmental Fund study says there are probably 10 million illegal aliens working in the United States today. There are about 12 million Americans of working age who are unemployed.

Only a handful of illegal aliens are being arrested and deported. The Immigration and Nationalization Service launched "Operation Jobs" and picked up thousands of illegal aliens working at jobs paying more than the minimum wage in Chicago, Houston, Dallas, Denver, Detroit, Newark, New York and Los Angeles. Some were making up to $10 an hour. Fifty illegal aliens earning from $7 to $9 an hour were arrested at an auto parts business near Chicago. Another 58 making $6 an hour were arrested at a San Francisco computer manufacturing plant. And yet, another 34 making $7.35 an hour were arrested at a Denver meat packing plant.

These were all industrial and urban or city jobs. Thousands upon thousands more illegal aliens are working agriculture in the United States.

Aliens Plan Civil Uprising

A special research organization in Washington, D.C., employing retired FBI and CIA agents known as the Business Environment Risk Index Service is predicting that guerrilla warfare led by communist agents and involving black and Hispanic gangs will attack white middle class businesses — a change from the ghetto-burnings of the past when blacks attacked blacks in Watts and Detroit and Newark and elsewhere.

The planned attacks on white middle class business will result in tremendous property damage and loss, and many casualties. They will have to be put down by government force. They are expected to be more than local police forces can handle.

The well known international banker, Felix G. Rohatyn, was quoted in the *Washington Post* as predicting uprising in American cities. Rudolfo Acuna, a militant Chicano leader, says Hispanics in the American Southwest are preparing for a separatist movement like the one going on in French-speaking Canada. It will demand independence for land in Colorado, Utah and Nevada that the Hispanic separatists claim were stolen from Mexico. The movement will have the support of thousands of illegal aliens who will want squatters rights on the land.

And another Chicano militant leader, Carlos Fernandiz, says

this: "There will be uprising here, it is just a matter of time. We will create our own country with Spanish as our language. We will secede from the United States by force if necessary. The whole Southwest will become another Vietnam, mark my words."

These are dangerous threats to American security and they are all being directed from the Kremlin to weaken the United States internally, particularly in the Southwest, so that communist revolution sweeping north from Central America through Mexico can spill over into the United States with little resistance.

Communists Must Be Stopped In Central America

The United States must keep on helping El Salvador fight communism because if it and the rest of Central America falls to the communists we're going to have 15 to 20 million refugees from there pouring across the Rio Grande. And the communist revolutionaries will be right behind them or mixed in with them.

The liberals in Congress keep trying to cut off aid to El Salvador. They did that to Vietnam and Vietnam fell to the communists. They did that to Nicaragua and Nicaragua fell to the communists. Now if they do that to El Salvador and it falls to the communists, Central America will be just like Southeast Asia. . .first Vietnam fell, then Laos, then Cambodia. If El Salvador falls, we will see Guatemala go right after it, then Honduras and then Mexico itself.

There are **100 million people** living between the Rio Grande and the Panama Canal. If the communists take them over, there will be **15 million** or **20 million** of them who will pick up and walk to America. They won't be "boat people" because it is dry land all the way. Sometimes the Rio Grande is only ankle deep.

More than 10 per cent of the people of Southeast Asia became refugees after the communist takeover — most of them leaving by boat — the boat people. If 10 per cent of the 100 million people living between the Rio Grande and the Panama Canal become refugees, that's 10 million refugees.Chances are that more than that will become refugees because they won't need a boat to get out. . .they can walk. So it is more likely there will be 15 million to 20 million refugees pouring into the United States over the Rio Grande if El Salvador falls, toppling over the rest of Central America and Mexico along with it. They won't be boat people. They will be **feet people**.

What will we do with 15 to 20 million additional aliens in

Texas, California, New Mexico and Arizona? They won't speak English. They won't have jobs. They won't have homes. They won't have schools. They won't have anything. We will have to let them starve in the streets or we will have to support them and their children with our taxes. It will bankrupt the country!

That's what El Salvador means to America. If it falls, and if the rest of Central America and then Mexico fall with it, God help America because the refugees will bankrupt us!

If you think we have economic problems now, wait until then. The state of Texas already has been ordered by the courts to provide free education for the children of illegal aliens. Now just add a few million more kids to that tax load and they will just have to shut down the schools in Texas.

The border patrol doesn't stand a chance. There are more government security officers guarding the buildings in Washington D.C., than there are guarding the American border.

The trouble in El Salvador is not with the anti-communist government there. The trouble is imported. . .directly from the Soviet Union through Cuba and Nicaragua to El Salvador. The goal is to take not just El Salvador but all of Central America and then Mexico and its oil fields for communism If that causes 15 or 20 million impoverished refugees who can't speak English to come pouring into the United States, the communists see that as just so much better. It will bankrupt the country and make the U.S. easier prey for the communists.

If El Salvador falls, the trouble — that is, the communist invasion — is going to move right on into the streets and suburbs of Houston and San Antonio and El Paso. It will be on the doorsteps in San Diego and Los Angeles. It will be the chief neighborhood activity in Tucson and Phoenix and Albuquerque and Santa Fe.

That's what's going to happen if we let El Salvador fall. El Salvador is not another Vietnam. It's not all that far away. There is no ocean between us and El Salvador. El Salvador is a Christian country, not a Buddhist country like Vietnam. El Salvador has plenty of poor people, all right, but not as many nor as poor as those in Vietnam. El Salvador has some industry, a sound agriculture economy — at least until the communists began to destroy it — several major cities, a modern transportation and utilities system in most urban areas. It's not like Vietnam. Those who try to compare it with Vietnam for propaganda purposes don't know what they are talking about. They have never been to El Salvador, or if they have, then they are lying and know it.

And remember this. The people of El Salvador voted, not for communism, but for conservative government leadership. By continuing to criticize our allies in El Salvador, the liberals in Congress are lending credibility, respectability and the implication of normal human virtues to godless communist terrorists who are murdering and destroying everyone and everything they can get their hands on.

And **media image-making** has been substituted for intelligent and substantive discussion on the issue of El Salvador. Instead of sensible debate on El Salvador's progress toward some kind of democracy, the media concentrates on reports of how many non-combatants have been killed in the communist revolution there. This is the deliberate work of a worldwide communist disinformation campaign meant to persuade the public opinion in the United States to abandon El Salvador and the Congress to quit helping this Christian anti-communist nation locked in a mortal struggle with the forces of godless communism.

Banks Losing Mexican Bet

While communists control the giant government bureaucracy in Mexico, several American banks have bet their battle for survival on the fate of Mexico.

Now what I'm about to reveal is not news in Mexico. . .it has been printed in some of the Mexico City newspapers, but it will be news to most Americans and especially to stockholders in certain big American banks which have made loans to Mexico that now total more than half the stockholders' equity or holdings in some of the banks.

Mexico has devalued the peso again in an effort to stay solvent. The fabled Mexican oil reserves have failed to pay off because of the worldwide drop in the price of oil. As a result, Mexico is troubled financially and its bureaucracy is still in the grip of a communist hierachy. Many American banks are in deep trouble financially because of big loans they have made to Mexico. I'm going to name those banks, the amount of money they have loaned to Mexico, and then more importantly, **the percentage** of stockholders' equity the loan represents.

Here they are:

Bank of America in San Francisco, $2.5 billion representing 59.1 per cent of the stockholders' investment in the bank; Citicorp, New York, $2.8 billion, 59.8 per cent of the stockholders' investment in the bank; Chase Manhattan, this is the David Rockefeller bank in New York, $1.5 billion, 46.5 per cent of shareholders' equity; Manufacturer's Hanover of

New York, $1.7 billion, **70.2** per cent. . .that's quite a bet on Mexico for the bank's stockholders; Chemical Bank of New York, $1.4 billion and an astounding **73 per cent** of stockholders' equity, the highest of any of the banks. . .**nearly three-fourths of the bank's value sunk in Mexican loans**; Continental of Chicago — this is the bank that got in trouble over the Penn Square failure in Oklahoma City and fired its petroleum loan advisor — $650 million, or 38.5 per cent of shareholders' equity — now in Mexico.

Continental would have failed if it had not been bailed out to the tune of several billion dollars by the Federal Deposit Insurance Corp. (taxpayer money) and several of its top executives were forced to resign as part of the deal.

Now here are some Texas banks' figures. Texas has the longest common border with Mexico of any state and does a lot of loan business across the border: Republic Bank of Dallas, $323 million, 37 per cent. . .**the highest loan amount and stockholders' equity share of any Texas bank loan to Mexico**; Texas Commerce of Houston, $302 million and 36.4 per cent, a close second behind Republic; Inter-First of Dallas, $199 million and 17.8 per cent; First City Bank of Houston, $194 million and 21.7 per cent of shareholders' equity to Mexico; Mercantile of Dallas, $120 million and 22.6 per cent; and Southwest Bank of Houston, $112 million and 30.2 per cent.

The big New York, Chicago and San Francisco banks have a total of $10.5 billion on loan to Mexico and the Texas banks have a paltry $1.2 billion loaned out to the **peso paradise**. Will they ever get it back? If I were a stockholder in those banks — and I'm not — I would at least ask about it.

The point of all this is that Mexico is threatened with more communist revolution from across its border with Guatemala; millions of its unemployed are flooding into the United States, some of them communist agents; Mexican militants are claiming the whole of the Southwest, saying it was taken illegally from Mexico in 1848 as a result of the Mexican American War; the Mexican government has many communists entrenched in its bureaucracy. . .and American banks and investors are up to their greenbacks in hot water down there. Let's hope the Mexicans don't say "adios, amigos" to them.

Mexico is trying to appease the communist revolutionaries in Central America and elsewhere in the region in order to protect its own oil resources.

Mexico has "recognized" the communist revolutionaries in El Salvador as a "legitimate" political interest there and has made overtures to "negotiate" a peace settlement. This is the same kind of mistake President Carter made when he betrayed Somoza in Nicaragua and then supported the socialization of business and agriculture in El Salvador — an attempt to coddle and mollify the communists by embracing their professed ideals. *It doesn't work.*

Mexico is running scared. It correctly sees the growing and better organized communist armies in the region as machetes aimed at its own vulnerable country. The Soviet goal for a long time has been to seize control of the oil fields and offshore oil potential of Mexico. No amount of waffling or conciliation or negotiation is going to change that goal. Nicaragua and El Salvador are small potatoes, just sideshows, compared with the coming communist storm against Mexico for its oil.

Mexico correctly discerns the divided political opinion in the United States that not only prevents a full-scale effort to rally Central and Latin America against communism but in fact reduces the chances of saving it at all. That's why it is doing everything within its power to cut its own deal with the communists and has shown only limited interest in President Reagan's Caribbean Initiative Plan. The Mexicans simply don't believe the United States has the political or military will to resist communism in the region.

Out of fashion as the domino theory may be — although it worked in Southeast Asia with the fall to communism of South Vietnam, Cambodia and Laos — the communist violence in Central America is aimed at toppling all the countries there right into Mexico.

Here is what will happen if El Salvador falls:

Guatemala, already torn by communist-inspired violence and strife, would be attacked along with Honduras in a series of invasions and turbulent events that the communists would insist on calling "civil wars." Mexico would be sucked inexorably into the conflict and to some extent already has been as many bandits calling themselves "guerrillas" have long been operating in southern Mexico, threatening oil facilities there.

Mexico has an armed force of perhaps 150,000 effectives but it has no combat experience, it is ill equipped, it is poorly led by a relatively weak and sadly incompetent and corrupt officers corps. It's training has largely been along the lines of conventional warfare and it is simply not prepared to fight a war against guerrillas. It has not prepared a counter-insurgency unit or a special forces unit such as the Green Berets to effectively oppose guerrillas and/or terrorists.

Mexico doesn't really trust the United States and it is likely that it would not fight a war against communist guerrillas. Mexico has a "macho" feeling about its national dignity, independence and sovereignty. The anti-American feeling in Mexico dates back to the Texas war for independence, the Mexican War of 1848 and accumulated other slights and affronts to Mexico, both real and imagined, over the years. It is hesitant to become dependent upon the U.S. for anything, including defense, for fear of losing dignity and independence. This limits Mexico's options when the time comes to defend itself. The United States would like to keep the guerrillas as distant from the Rio Grande as possible. We won't exactly be able to march troops into Mexico like we can into Texas.

This is why suggestions about a "North American community" or "mutual defense treaty" or "American common market" gets such a negative reaction in Mexico City. Respect and dignity are essential to Mexicans for any kind of mutual relationship from the personal to the national level. Mexico simply feels like it hasn't gotten that from the United States.

Aside from the diplomatic psychology, the very real matter of money in the form of trade between the United States and Mexico is becoming one of the controversial issues between the two countries in the 1980s. Mexico is the United States' third largest trading partner behind Canada and Japan.

But differences in commercial policy and how b usiness is done already pose big questions about the future of the trade. Mexico declined to sign an international agreement on General Tariffs and Trade and this is certain to be an eventual obstacle.

So far as the United States is concerned, Mexico is the source of two serious problems: illegal aliens and drugs.

While the U.S. considers the aliens a "problem," Mexico considers them to be a natural circumstance and would like to have them assured some share of the U.S. labor market. Mexico also has a paternal interest in the human and labor rights of its nationals in the U.S. whether or not they are here legally, while the U.S. policy toward them is to deport them if found and deny them protection otherwise. This is already a big obstacle between warm relations for the two countries.

Then there is drugs. Mexico is the largest supplier of marijuana to the United States and there are simply no statistics available to determine the multi-billion dollars estimated value of the traffic.

There is evidence that entire regions of Mexico are devoted to raising marijuana and poppies (a source of opium and heroin). The cultivation of illicit drug crops in the Oaxaca area exceeds the lawful cultivation of food crops by more than seven billion pesos! Food crops there in a recent harvest amounted to 3.6 billion pesos compared with drug crops estimated at 10 billion pesos.

Mexico has rarely cooperated with U.S. enforcement officials and United Nations directives to combat the drug traffic and drug crop cultivation and there is no indication it is truly being brought under control.

Mexico also is in deep trouble because it has the fastest growing population of any country in the world. It has grown from 30 million to 68 million in the past 25 years. This helps explain the flood of aliens into the United States and many of them are bringing their Marxist allegiance with them. Mexico has turned to Marxism, helped along by its leaders and by a strong radical element in the Catholic Church.

One of Mexico's best friends is Fidel Castro. When Castro visited Mexico for confidential meetings, the Cuban dictator was given a 21-gun salute and full honors as a chief of state.

The radical element of the Catholic Church is taking control because nearly two-thirds of all the Catholic priests and nuns in Latin America are said to be Marxists supporting terrorism and revolution. Mexico's Bishop Mendez Arceo has said: *"The Kingdom of Heaven can come about in our day only by Marxism."*

Mexico's politics, Marxist-style religion and the oil have done little to solve its economic problems. The Mexican peso was devalued by a whopping 28 per cent. The price of its heavier crude oil was cut. Inter-bank peso trading was suspended. Foreign investment is declining, interest-free loans to Mexico by the World Bank are being phased out and the interest on supply mortgage money and corporation loans rose to about 40 per cent.

R.E. McMaster Jr., a commodity advisor and financial consultant who was reared in South Texas and who has worked with and lived among Mexicans and those of Mexican descent nearly all his life, had this to say in a news letter to his customers and subscribers:

"Having studied this problem for over a decade, it is this writer's firm opinion that there is no greater challenge facing the U.S. citizens in the Southwest region of this country over the next few years — not the economy, not the climate, not inflation, not the Russians, not the federal government — Mexico is the threat. . .

"Investors should avoid Mexico totally! With an eye toward

the long-term consequences of this rapidly emerging problem, real estate investments in the Southwest U.S. should be carefully selected, probably minimized, protected, and perhaps even sold if located in the hotly disputed lands."

McMaster charges that the "undermining of the Southwest's social order is already underway" by the flood of Mexican immigrants, most entering illegally, including those with Marxist sentiments. He says the "four phases" of terrorism have already been "kicked into gear" and that the subversive apparatus has been established for disruption of government in the Southwest. McMaster states:

"**Next will come increasing acts of terrorism. This will be followed by guerrilla warfare and finally a full-scale revolutionary war, as young Mexicans, with nothing to lose, as indoctrinated Marxists, with a hatred for the U.S., attempt to recapture the lands which they believe rightfully belong to Mexico.**

"**These Mexican terrorists will attempt to achieve the three main goals of terrorism: (1) Show the people in the border states that the U.S. government is unable to protect them against terrorists; (2) Provoke U.S. authorities into overreacting against the terrorists which will further alienate the Hispanic people from the government; (3) Overthrow state governments and U.S. institutions in the border states, making use of propaganda and chaos.**"

Mexico's long dominant ruling party, in power for half a century and little short of a dictatorship, has shown no inclination to challenge Marxist guerrilla activity. Instead it has been openly supporting the guerrillas in El Salvador.

It is preposterous for the U.S. to pretend that Mexico could be a neutral, impartial intermediary for settling the Central America dispute. It has too many Marxist tendencies, has cuddled up too closely to Castro, has been ineffective in controlling illegal guerrilla activities within its borders, has been anti-American in its official pontificating for years while looking for someone or something to blame its economic troubles on and is in fact a critically weak nation.

No, we cannot afford to look to Mexico to stop the communist guerrillas from coming through that country on their way to the United States. It is too weak politically, to corrupt nationally, and simply too unfriendly toward the United States to rely on.

The Big Oil Lie
When oil prices were booming in the late 1970s and Mexico

found new oil reserves, world economists and bankers became convinced that the oil would solve Mexico's economic and social problems. And it appeared to be doing just that for a few years, but like Poland, Mexico's success was being subsidized by massive amounts of foreign debt, about $70 billion worth borrowed from private firms, public corporations and government agencies from throughout the world but largely from the United States and Western European economies.

Mexico is running out of oil, not building up fabulous reserves.

The communist bureaucrats or commucrats who run much of the Mexican government, including the oil industry which was "nationalized" in 1938 as Pemex, have exaggerated the amount of oil reserves in Mexico and borrowed billions of dollars based on the exaggerations.

Or let me put it this way — they lied about the oil and borrowed money on the lie.

The truth is that Mexico has been running out of oil since 1921 and the "fabulous reserves" proclaimed by the Mexican commucrats in the 1970s are not fabulous after all.

The latest survey of Mexican oil, based on the best information available that was assembled by non-Mexican geologists, is reported in a recent edition of "*World Petroleum Resources and Reserves*" published in Boulder, Colorado, and it reports the following:

• Mexico is producing about 2.75 million barrels of oil per day but only exporting 1.5 million barrels.

• Proved reserves of oil, meaning oil within known fields that possibly can be recovered with existing technology if capital becomes available, total 26.5 billion barrels of oil.

• *Inferred reserves, meaning field growth or oil generally bordering known fields that possibly could be recovered in the future total 21 billion barrels.*

• Undiscovered resources, meaning oil that Pemex claims is there, totals 50 billion barrels.

It is some 10 billion barrels of "inferred reserves" that don't exist and all of the 50 billion barrels of "undiscovered resources" that the U.S. government (meaning you and I as taxpayers), American and international bankers, and the United Nations' International Monetary Fund are banking on as a dream that may come true, or may become a nightmare.

Mexico's foreign debt is $85.5 billion. When Mexico announced in August, 1982, that it could not make scheduled payments of some $3 billion on its foreign debt because declining world oil prices had trimmed anticipated revenue, the U.S. "loaned" Mexico $32 billion in emergency funds, including $1 billion in advance oil payments. The International Monetary Fund promised Mexico additional support, including another $8.5 billion in U.S. tax money approved by Congress late in 1983 just before the Christmas holiday adjournment of Congress. That was the U.S. part of the IMF promise of some $32 billion headed for Latin America and communist points East.

Mexico has made a mess of its oil business despite the supposed "oil boom" of recent years. Mexican oil production began in 1904, hit a peak in 1921, declined until 1938 when all oil investment was "nationalized" and the decline continued until new reserves were discovered from 1968 to 1974 when oil was once again exported.

The American "loan" and the IMF "loan" are based on future production of Mexican oil but the more recent geology reports and analysis are not encouraging. They read like this:

"The belief in an almost limitless Mexican petroleum resource has recently become subject to geological and engineering analysis. Such analysis suggest a lowering of the reported magnitude of Mexican oil."

And like this: **"The Chicontepec reservoirs (the new reserves) are well-sorted by tightly cemented sandstones that were deposited in ancient bars and channels. Wells in these widespread sandstones are less prolific than those in other Mexican areas."**

And like this: **"Individual offshore wells (other new reserves) were found to be highly prolific producers, but offshore crude is usually heavier and contains more sulfur than most onshore crudes."**

What all this is saying if put in English is that Mexico doesn't have near as much oil as its communist-oriented bureaucrats are claiming and what it does have is not very good quality oil. That's evident from the foul haze it leaves smothering Mexico City during rush hours when burned in auto engines there. Its lead and sulfur content is so high that its giving Mexico City residents blood poisoning just from breathing the exhaust.

The U.S. Geological Survey and the U.S. Department of Energy have made a field-by-field survey to estimate proven Mexican oil reserves and came up with the figure of 26.5 billion barrels. The **commucrats** running Pemex claim 48 billion barrels. The discrepancy includes the aforementioned Chicontepec region where Pemex claims 10.9 billion barrels that the U.S. agencies can't or won't confirm.

The missing 10.9 billion barrels is kindly included in the 21 billion barrel figure for "inferred reserves." The World Petroleum Resources and Reserves Report says of this inference: "It may be realized in the long-term from much additional drilling and subsequent field growth but is not currently proved."

When the dust settles from all the beating around the bush by Mexican communist bureaucrats and U.S. Government geologists and Energy Department bureaucrats, it can be plainly seen that the Mexicans have lied about and exaggerated about their oil reserves. Uncle Sam and the IMF bought the lie for a bale of money. Don't expect to see it or the oil flowing back this way anytime soon.

When oil prices began to fall from more than $40 per barrel to the vicinity of $30 at the outset of the 1980s, it became clear that Mexico would be unable to pay the foreign debts when they came due. With a worldwide recession going on in the early 1980s, banks and international financial cartels were more reluctant to refinance such debts as those run up by Mexico by the old traditional methods of rolling over old loans and especially by extending new loans. Mexico faced the painful problem of taking away goods and services from the average Mexican citizen and selling them in international markets in order to pay the debts and interest when they came due. The average Mexican citizen could ill afford such government manipulation which would lower an already low Mexican standard of living — the same problem Poland faced.

In both Mexico and in Poland the result of such financial maneuvering would be social chaos, fueling the already smoldering discontent in both nations.

Mexico's so-called "social safety valve" has been illegal emigration into the United States but Americans grappling with their own economic difficulties have demanded a curb to this cheap labor which they believe take jobs from them. Should that safety valve be closed, the communist agitation in Mexico would increase rapidly and its eventual conquest by revolution or by cooperation with regular communist troops invading from Central America would be virtually certain.

Mexico And The Church

Marxism is growing stronger in Mexico with the help of liberal segments of the Roman Catholic Church. In recent elections, Bishop Sergio Mendez Arceo, known as "The Red Bishop" of Cuernavaca, preached "that one could vote for a Marxist party" and added:

"What's even more important, the dialectical variety of Marxist thought allows for an individual to be faithful to Christ and be a good Marxist at the same time."

This is pure heresy, intended to dupe and mislead those not well-grounded in Holy Scripture or not familiar with the writings and teachings of Karl Marx into believing the two opposites — Christianity and Marxism — can be compatible.

The Vatican representative in Mexico denounced Bishop Arceo's statement and said very plainly: "A convinced Marxist cannot be a Christian, just as a Christian cannot be a Marxist because Marxism goes against God."

The point is that the communists know that despite all of Mexico's economic and social problems, they must destroy the Christian church in Mexico by dividing and conquering it if they expect to win Mexico over to Marxism. In Mexico, as in the rest of the remaining free world, the church — not the military or the politicians — stands as the main barrier to any communist takeover, and the communists know it.

The relationship between Mexico and the United States has been compared with the relationship between Poland and the Soviet Union in that the economies of both Poland and Mexico are in serious trouble and deeply in debt; that both Poland and Mexico have lost territory to their larger neighbors, and that the U.S. may well have to send troops into Mexico to put down an armed revolution or a buildup for a communist invasion of the U.S. on the grounds of national security.

The upshot of all this unpleasant business with Mexico is that the United States could find itself in the awkward position of having to commit an act of war against Mexico to save it from communist invasion and conquest. Because of our many differences with Mexico, we could not blithely send an expeditionary force into Southern Mexico to defend its oil fields even if there was political support for such a move, which doesn't seem very likely in light of the controversy over El Salvador. The indications from Mexico are that it fears the United States as much or more than the communists. Mexico would not likely invite our military intervention , at least not until it was too late.

Rather than wait until the communists are on the Rio Grande, would Washington intervene in Mexico uninvited? If we did, would we be fighting the Mexican people as well as the Soviet-Cuba directed communists? Should the communists reach the Rio Grande and begin excursions into Texas and the Southwest, would Mexico be considered a safe sanctuary for them, like Manchuria was across the Yalu River in Korea? Is

America content to wait until those questions are forced upon us by communist aggression or are we willing to do anything about stopping communism now?

All these diplomatic problems we have with Mexico now — trade, drugs, immigration, oil — will be what the lawyers call "moot questions" should the communists openly take over Mexico. Our problem then will be how to defend ourselves, not how to deal delicately with the Mexicans, should we last that long.

Our problem now is when and where to take a stand against communism. We have been lulled into a false sense of security by our leaders, our news media, our clergy, our educators, our intellectuals and our other liberal thinkers and expounders who have persuaded us that communism is no longer a danger to the world, to free people. Now here it is on our doorstep preparing to come into the house.

Decision time is upon us. It's going to be too late when the communists come across the Rio Grande in force and fighting breaks out in the streets of Houston and San Antonio and Dallas and Phoenix and Los Angeles to wonder "how did this happen?" The purpose of this book is to tell you how it is happening right now, while there is still some time, precious little time, to do something about it short of taking up personal weapons in individual and disorganized attempts to defend ourselves, our homes and our families.

We have been lulled into "a communist state of mind" in the United States. We have been led into a blind alley of apathy and indifference and unconcern, where we can be trapped without a way out by the reality of brutal communism crushing this country like Poland has been crushed, like Nicaragua was crushed, like El Salvador is being crushed.

The way to peace is not marching down the street with banners asking for unilateral disarmaments and one-way nuclear freezes. That's exactly what our enemy wants us to do.

The way to peace is by faith in God through Christ that our leaders will have the courage to do what they must do, however unpopular politically, to strengthen our country so it can resist the advance and invasion of militant, godless communism.

We must support a strong national defense posture. We must support our friends and allies already engaged in military battle with the communists. We must support those who stand for a strong and free America. We pray to God that you can find in your heart support for this Christian Crusade ministry and its continuing work to rally this nation to oppose the evil force of atheistic communism that would rob us of our liberties and our country.

Chapter 7

WHAT WENT WRONG IN NICARAGUA

As the disillusioned and the defeated escape from communist Nicaragua, their stories have begun to piece together an answer for what went wrong with the 1979 revolution there that they thought would be "different" from all other revolutions.

When the Somoza government fell to the so-called "Sandinista" revolution in July, 1979, the people of Nicaragua had high hopes for a new Nicaragua in which democracy would prevail and human rights would be respected and the poor, at last, would be uplifted.

Except for the presence of what appeared to be a minority of communists in the revolution at the time, there had seemed to be a broad support — the business community had staged three crippling strikes against Somoza in January 1978; a wide range of non-Marxist political parties and labor unions had helped the revolution; the Roman Catholic Church had issued pastoral letters opposing Somoza.

Never had such near-ideal conditions existed for a truly successful "non-Marxist" revolutionary government to be established in Latin America.

What went wrong?

The liberal, leftist American news media contends unfriendly U.S. policies toward the new Sandinista government "pushed it" into the Soviet orbit. That's all wet, a pure media myth dreamed up by the liberals on the *New York Times* and the *Washington Post* news and editorial staffs.

For one thing, the Carter administration was hardly

131

unfriendly, having been the main provider of funds to the Sandinistas, with an early grant of some $75 million. Other Western democratic nations helped with money and materials for restructuring the new government. It was the United States and other Western countries who had sent the most aid to Nicaragua during the disastrous earthquake there which destroyed downtown Managua late in the Somoza regime. There was no ill will toward the Sandinistas to drive them into the Soviet orbit, as the news media still claims.

In fact, it was during this very "honeymoon" period, in May 1980, that the Sandinistas signed an agreement of mutual support with the Communist Party of the Soviet Union in which Nicaragua pledged to endorse Soviet foreign policy including the invasion of Afghanistan. There were no hostile Western forces, political or military, harrassing Nicaragua at that time. There was no "contra" or anti-revolutionary force of disillusioned Nicaraguans operating anywhere within the country at that time.

What went wrong first was that as soon as the shooting ended in July 1979, thousands of communist Cubans arrived in Nicaragua as "teachers" and "good-will advisors." They immediately began agitating against freedom of the press and what they "taught" was the Marxist rhetoric of "class struggle" against the United States. By March, 1980, the Nicaragua Council of State, which was the national congress, where Marxists originally had only one-third of the seats, was changed by government decree to give the Sandinistas two-thirds of the seats, arbitrarily ousting business and middle class representatives. That's when things began to really go wrong.

The now Marxist-dominated Sandinista Party was truly Communist, it reneged on its promise of free elections and announced the party would "select" the best leaders from among "the vanguard of the people," meaning themselves, the Communists. It was Moscow, with its phalanx of Cuban advisors and teachers and revolutionary infiltrators that pulled Nicaragua into the Soviet orbit, not the United States that pushed it there, no matter how hard the *New York Times* tries to make the American people believe otherwise.

Today, five years after the revolution, Nicaragua is on the brink of civil war, society is divided, "contras" are fighting within the country to regain control of the original revolution now lost to communism, a Castro-style regime is running the country and the long-ago dreamed of "new society" is in ashes.

Nicaragua has taken the old worn-out path of Marxist-

Leninism which mistakenly believes that the evils of this world can be remedied by overturning what communists call "oppressive socio-economic structures of society," meaning private ownership of the means of production, that is, capitalism. If communists can defeat the sources that defend and support capitalism — chiefly, the United States — then oppression will end and utopia will begin, they claim.

The inherent weakness of the Marxist-Leninist-Communist theory is that man, not God, will deliver salvation to the poor and oppressed. Marxists look upon the United States as Christians look upon Satan. Marxists set themselves up as the "new gods" to be worshipped by the masses as the only ones who can deliver salvation. And as with all gods, one must either be for or against with no middle ground allowed. In worshipping the "new gods" of communism, one must surrender individualism, private property, religion and independence.

That's what went wrong in Nicaragua — not American hostility but Marxist demands for state worship by the people.

Once in control of the Nicaraguan government, the Marxists then began trying to spread the world-wide communist revolution into nearby El Salvador. It was in defense of El Salvador and in containment of the communist aggression and subversion increasing in Honduras and Guatemala that the United States began supporting the Contras, increasing aid to El Salvador and mining Nicaraguan waters to slow down the flow of Soviet arms into the Central American hot spot.

The American Congressmen opposing President Reagan's assistance to the anti-communist nations in Central America threatened by Communist Nicaragua don't understand the Red Messianic nature of communism, the "new gods." The Congressmen go to Central America, hear the old stories of poverty and oppression, and accept blame on behalf of America. They can't grasp that the Nicaraguans thought they had taken care of their own problem with the Sandinista revolution only to see it subverted by Marxism. The Congress is at least five years behind in its thinking on Central America and from its actions and statements is light years behind understanding communism.

President Reagan understands. He has called the Soviet Union an "evil empire" and he means it and hasn't retracted it and the Soviets have given him no reason to do so. Reagan, a Christian, understands that the "new gods" of communism are trying to overthrow not only economic rivals but the very God of the Bible. This is Satan's only goal and purpose, to overthrow God. The "new gods" of communism are mere surrogates for Satan, serving his purpose here on earth.

This is the Satanic nature of communism at work in unhappy Nicaragua. This is the continuing preview of the buildup toward the God versus Satan tribulation period and the coming battle of Armageddon.

Nicaragua is just another staging point on the way to Armageddon. It has become another Satanic base for communism. That's what went wrong with Nicaragua.

Pro-Red Traitors in Our Government?

You may have read about or heard about a letter from 10 Congressmen written not long ago to the communists who rule Nicaragua.

It was addressed to "**Dear Commandante** Daniel Ortega," who is the communist in charge there. It was **anti-American** in both tone and content. It started out apologizing for the fact that the Reagan administration has been helping to fight communism in Nicaragua and elsewhere in Central America by supplying arms and money to Nicaraguan freedom fighters known as "contras" trying to get their country back from the communists.

It praised the communists for "opening up the political process" by planning elections, although none have been held yet — compared with two in the last two years in El Salvador. It said "we support your decision to reduce press censorship." Two weeks later the communists censored 65 per cent of the newspaper *La Prensa*, so much censorship that the publisher cancelled that day's edition. It happens all the time. It said the communists can establish an example of historical importance in Central America. I guess that's true if they mean communist revolution is the example and communist terror is important.

The letter said the 10 Congressmen would like nothing more than friendship with the communists based on what they called "true equality, self-determination and mutual good will." They asked for negotiations to settle the war in Central America and condemned those who would obstruct such negotiations — meaning President Reagan.

I think it is only right that the 10 Congressmen who wrote this **communist-embracing letter of appeasement** have their names "printed for the record" so there won't be any doubt who we are talking about. They were Jim Wright of Texas, Michael Barnes of Maryland, Bill Alexander of Arkansas, Matthew McHugh of New York, Robert Torricelli of New

Jersey, Edward P. Boland of Massachusetts, Stephen Solarz of New York, David R. Obey of Wisconsin, Robert Garcia of New York and Lee Hamilton of Indiana.

The Soviet adviser to the dictator of Nicaragua rejoiced when he read this sentence from the Congressmen's letter: "We have been, and remain, **opposed to United States support** for military action directed against the people or **government** of Nicaragua."

The KGB man knows that if it hadn't been for U.S. support of military action against the communist government of Nicaragua that the communists would already have taken El Salvador and been far up the road into Mexico toward the Rio Grande.

These Congressmen talk about "covert action" by the U.S. government against the communists in Nicaragua like it was some kind of **sin to fight for freedom.** Did they ever hear of the French underground fighting against the Nazis in World War II? That was covert action. Have they heard of the Afghan mountain guerrillas fighting against the Soviet invaders in Afghanistan? That's covert action. In fact, when the communists took Nicaragua in the first place, that started out as covert action. It seems like nobody declares war anymore because that would involve treason, censorship and trading with the enemy.

We didn't declare war in Korea but we did a lot of bombing and fighting. We didn't declare war in Vietnam but we bombed Hanoi and mined Haiphong harbor. This is the real, old evil world we are living in, Congressmen. You had better forget politics every now and then and think about freedom instead.

If the United States ever get as weak as the backbone of those 10 Congressmen when it comes to standing up for freedom and against tyranny, for Christ and against godless communism, then all of us may wind up writing to **"Dear Commandante"** one of these days: asking him to either let us out of jail or let us visit a loved one who is in jail.

Along with that evidence of communist sympathizing Congressmen trying to help the Reds in Nicaragua, there is also evidence that American "churchmen," under the banner of the National Council of Churches also are playing the game of "we love the communists the most."

Why is the National Council of Churches still supporting the Marxist government of Nicaragua when the original supporters from the United States have since backed out?

Council spokesmen claim the council is only supporting what is called a "literacy" program to the tune of some $200,000 or more. The fact is that the literacy program is nothing more than a communist political propaganda program designed to brainwash those who opposed the Marxist revolution in the first place.

The tactics are the same. Those to be brainwashed are required to attend classes for hours at a time to the point of exhaustion. They are forced to listen to communist indoctrination speeches, and to accept and read communist propaganda literature and to watch communist propaganda films. This is the program that money from the NCC is going to support in Nicaragua.

The NCC has not come out against the suppression of religion and freedom of speech and press in Nicaragua. The council has not come out against the abuse of human rights there, or said one thing about the Marxist massacres of the poor Miskito Indians and the removal of survivors from their ancestral homes. The NCC is aiding and abbeting the Marxist rulers of Nicaragua by helping to finance their propaganda program through a misnamed **literacy class!**

The NCC argues in its defense that it only began helping the Marxists because President Carter's administration gave them $75 million in 1979 in a foolish scheme to prevent the Marxists from taking aid funneled through Cuba from the Soviet Union.

That didn't work. **The Marxists took the American money and laughed!** Certain American labor unions also sent money to the Marxists for the same mistaken reason that Carter did.

But when it became clear — as many who had opposed the aid had predicted — that the Marxists not only had turned Nicaragua into a police state but also had begun **exporting communist revolution to El Salvador,** the U.S. government and the unions quit sending aid, but the NCC didn't.

The NCC is such a big ecclessiastical bureaucracy that its right hand rarely knows what its left hand is doing. Several denominations of the NCC have been infiltrated and are now being dominated by leftist liberals who are in sympathy with the phony liberation theology being promoted by Marxists in Central America. This is why the NCC continues to aid the revolutionary Marxist government there just as it has in Zimbabwe-Rhodesia for years. If the NCC is not **communist to the core,** it has to be ranked as one of communism's most avid friends and financial supporters.

The Marxists in Nicaragua are very grateful to the **National Council of Churches** for financial support. The Nicaraguan ministry of education had this to say about it:

136

With the literacy drive we propose **to contribute** *to achieving a greater understanding of the revolutionary process and a more effective inculcation of the tasks required to* **advance the revolution."**

Contribute to and advance the revolution, the Marxists say. Think about that next time the collection plate comes by!

Every American city is now within a short flying time of communist missiles and jet aircraft bases in Nicaragua.

The missiles can strike in minutes and jet bombers can follow up within a matter of hours. Armored cars and personnel carriers can drive from Nicaragua to Texas in two days. Heavy tanks can follow up in a few more days. Nicaragua is on the mainland of the continent, unlike the island of Cuba.

It is a sign of tragic unwillingness of the American people to accept the reality of the communist danger that we are faced with Soviet troops in the Western Hemisphere. Soviet naval ships manuevering off our coast. Soviet equipment pouring into communist Nicaragua, communist guerrillas openly attacking while stating they are fighting a widespread regional war. . .and the concern in Washington is what America is doing wrong!

John F. Kennedy would turn over in his grave if he could see today how his beloved party's successors in Congress have betrayed the policies he once risked war to establish in Latin America. He blockaded Cuba to stop more Soviet missiles from going in there. Americans cheered! Reagan approves a few mines in Nicaraguan waters and you would think he had bombed Pearl Harbor!

The fact is that for the last five years communist Nicaragua has systematically built a communist base and guerrilla movement for attacking its neighbors in El Salvador and Honduras and for suppressing the civilian population to crush an objections or dissent. These policies have not come from Managua, they have come directly from Moscow.

If you talk to people from Honduras or Costa Rica or Guatemala — to say nothing of El Salvador — they will tell you that they are terrified of the scale of the Soviet buildup in Nicaragua. I was in Costa Rica speaking recently and our Christian Crusade writer Bill Sampson was in El Salvador previously and we both saw it and heard about it.

The Soviet buildup has made Nicaragua the most powerful military force in Central America. The communist dictatorship of Nicaragua has more airfields for jet aircraft, more artillery pieces and a larger army than all their neighbors combined.

They have the only tanks in the region.

In this setting, with five years of communist dictatorship increasing the pressure on the people, with press censorship, with the Catholic Church now opposing the dictatorial regime, with increasing anger against the dictatorship, with thousands of people fleeing Nicaragua prepared to fight for their freedom, our Congress tells us that we are to look only at El Salvador and forget history.

Congress is acting like a policeman who comes upon a mugging and arrests the victim for fighting back.

There is a terrorist internationale in place in Nicaragua, composed of Soviet soldiers, Cuban soldiers, Bulgarian soldiers, North Vietnamese soldiers, North Korean soldiers and communist Nicaraguan mercenaries. And yet, the American news media is more concerned that the United States of America should be hailed before the world Court for mining Nicaraguan waters! The Soviet Union never goes before the World Court for shooting down civilian airliners and other murders, yet we are expected to submit to international — or I should say internationale — justice.

The admirers of John F. Kennedy seem to have forgotten that he once said:

"Let all our neighbors know that we shall join with them to oppose aggression or subversion anywhere in the Americas."

Are we to believe that all those foreign troops are in Nicaragua to get a suntan? Or was Kennedy wrong about defending this hemisphere from foreign aggression?

El Salvador and Honduras and such citizens of Nicaragua as the Miskito Indians are under illegal armed attack. In that setting, even under the Charter of the helpless United Nations, we Americans — meaning North, South and Central Americans — are entitled to take individual or collective defense measures necessary to protect lawful objectives, including the territorial and political integrity of El Salvador and the other countries in the regions.

Professor John Norton Moore of the University of Virginia Law School, an expert in international law, says such defense measures include both "overt and covert responses," which covers the mining of Nicaraguan waters to stop Soviet supplies from further disrupting the region.

When you have a nation like the Soviet Union that is in the business of selling destabilization of the peace, there is nothing wrong with stopping their inventory of chaos from coming in.

One of the lessons of Vietnam was that when we finally

138

mined Haiphong harbor in 1972 it had a tremendous impact on the North Vietnamese communists and led directly to the peace negotiations that ended the war in 1973. It was only when we betrayed our South Vietnamese allies after the peace was in effect by cutting off their military aid that the communists resumed the war and took Saigon (I'll never call it Ho Chi Minh City) in 1975.

While the liberal, leftist American news media and hysterical congressmen focus on what they think the United States is doing wrong in Central America, we should pause a moment for some perspective and look at the other side.

The Soviet Union has sent $112 million worth of arms to Nicaragua in just one year, all the way from Russia, halfway around the world. That $112 million is just for arms and other military equipment. It doesn't count the cost of training and support of the terrorist internationale brigade now encamped in Nicaragua directing the war against El Salvador and Honduras.

The United States spent $44 million in El Salvador one year and that includes everything right down to the food for the 55 military advisers we have there. That's our 55 compared with the 3,500 communist soldiers from many communist bloc countries stationed in Nicaragua.

The communist arms get to Nicaragua in ships. More communist ships docked in Nicaragua in the last year than in the previous 20 years.

In early 1985, the Soviet Union sent the aircraft carrier "Leningrad" to the Caribbean Sea along with a guided missile destroyer, a fleet oiler and a submarine to practice with the Cuban Navy for the first time in history. The Cubans went to sea in two frigates and a landing ship designed specifically for amphibious assaults. Together, the formidable Red Navy could put ashore a major assault force nearly anywhere around the circumference of the Gulf of Mexico, including the coastlines of five American states — Florida, Alabama, Mississippi, Lousiana and Texas.

The communist guerrillas have boasted repeatedly that they are fighting a regional war that has no national boundaries, that after El Salvador comes Guatemala; after Guatemala comes Honduras; after Honduras comes Mexico; after Mexico. . .guess what?

Fifty-five American advisers and a few mines in Nicaraguan waters are not going to stop them. And they are not kidding. They are quoted in the *New York Times* as to exactly what their plans are and what they are going to do, just as Hitler said what he was going to do, just as Lenin and Stalin said what they were going to do, just as Mao Tse-Tung said what he was going to do.

The American Congressmen who cheered the downfall of Anastasio Somoza in Nicaragua when the communists overthrew him now seem struck deaf, dumb and blind by what is happening there. They cannot bring themselves to criticize anything but the actions of the United States of America.

Congressman Tom Downey of New York called the Nicaraguan Freedom Fighters being supported by the United States — the "Contras" as they are known — he called them "thugs, thieves and brigands" for fighting against communism.

Washington Post Reporter Karen De Young, who engineered the journalistic attack on Somoza, now kindly describes the communist dictorship of Nicaragua as "a non-pluralistic socialism."

The Congress and the press are far behind reality. They look at the mad tyranny in Nicaragua as though it was still a revolution when in fact it long ago lost any right to be called that.

Recently when I was in Costa Rica, I went up into the mountains to interview "Commander Zero," the legendary military hero of the original revolution that overthrew Somoza. His real name is Eden Pastora. He was not a communist originally. He fought against Somoza because he believed then that the revolution he was leading was like the American Revolution against King George, that a better life of freedom would result. The communists took him over for awhile just like they did the rest of the revolution and corrupted it. Pastora fled into exile and has been fighting back against communism from there. He is only one of many, many of the original Nicaraguan revolutionaries who have fled communist Nicaragua after realizing the mistake they made in helping put the communists into power. They are leaders of the so-called "Contras" despised as "thugs, thieves and brigands" by Congressman Downey.

Congressman Downey and his colleagues turn a deaf ear to those people who are now crying out for help to regain their country for real democracy and true pluralism, not the phony stuff Reporter De Young writes about. These are the people who gave the original revolution its legitimacy and its soul before the communists wrestled power from them and forced them into exile:

"Commander Zero," Eden Pastora, ex-deputy defense minister.

Alfonso Robelo, member of the original Sandinista junta before communists forced their way into it, now in exile.

Arturo Cruz, ex-Sandinista ambassador to the United States, now in exile.

Jose Francisco Cardenal, former vice president, now in exile.

Edgard Macias, head of the Popular Social Christian Party, now in exile.

Jose Esteban Gonzales, head of the Nicaraguan Permanent Commission on Human Rights, now in exile.

Violeta Chamorro, wife of a slain Nicaraguan newspaper publisher, ex-member of the original junta.

Pedro Joaquin Chamorro Jr., son of the slain publisher and now a disillusioned former Sandinista supporter.

Humberto Belli, anti-Somoza editor of La Presna newspaper, now heavily censored by the communists.

Jaime Montealeger, ex-vice president of the original Sandinista Council of State.

Agustin Alfaro, ex-Sandinista consul general in New Orleans, now in exile.

Adolfo Calero, head of the Nicaraguan Conservative Party, now fighting along with the "Contra" forces on the Honduras-Nicaragua border.

Archbishop Obando Y Bravo, head of the Nicaraguan Catholic Church, former Sandinista supporter and now an outspoken critic of the communists. Only his church position and his popularity among the masses of Catholics in Nicaragua protects him from communist vengeance for now.

Carlos Coronel, ex-Sandinista minister of fisheries, now in exile.

Alvaro Taboada, ex-Sandinista ambassador to Ecuador, now in exile.

Francisco Flallos, ex-Sandinista ambassador to Geneva, now in exile.

Heraldo Montealegre, ex-Sandinista alternate governor of the World Bank, now in exile.

Steadman Fagoth, leader of the persecuted Miskito Indians, fled across the border into Honduras.

The list goes on and on, and grows daily as more and more Nicaraguans either flee the country or secretly or openly conspire with the Freedom Fighters in what they are now beginning to call the "Nuevolution," a contraction for "New Revolution," meaning the new anti-communist revolution.

To stop this "Nuevolution," the communists are conducting a campaign of terror inside Nicaragua as well as exporting communist insurrection outside its borders.

A CHRONOLOGY OF COLONIES FOR COMMUNISM
(1958-1984)
Cuba, 1958; South Vietnam, Laos, Cambodia, 1975; Angola, Mozambique, 1976; Ethiopia, South Yemen, 1977; Afghanistan, 1978; Grenada (until liberated), 1979; Nicaragua, 1980.

Who's Boss In Nicaragua Now?

When I visited Central America, the news there — news not being printed in America — was that Nicaragua is now under the control of six families known as the Marxist Mafia.

When Jimmy Carter was president, he abandoned America's long-time ally, Anastasio Somoza (just like he did the Shah of Iran) and gave a green light to the Marxists to takeover Nicaragua. They did just that and now the real rulers of Nicaragua are these people:

Family No. 1 — **Daniel and Umberto Saavedra.** Daniel is Junta coordinator and close friend of socialist President Mitterand of France. Umberto is commander-in-chief of the Army.

Family No. 2 — **The Guzman Cuadra brothers,** leftist aristocrats. Fernado is head of the National Development Bank; Gilberto is secretary-treasurer and Alvaro is assistant secretary of commerce.

Family No. 3 — **The Chamoro Clan.** Joaquin (uncle of the Guzman Cuadra boys) is minister of finance. His son is military chief of staff and his three daughters are each married to one of the junta leaders, a top security chief, and a high-ranking army officer.

Family No. 4 — **The Roman family.** Jaime Wheelock Roman is the head and a major property holder, much of it former Somoza property. Brother Ricardo is ambassador to the Soviet Union. Other relations are in charge of the radio ministry and the ministry of culture.

Family No. 5 — **The Ramirez Mercado mob.** Sergio is on the junta; brother Rogelio is Secretary of Municipal Affairs; Sergio's wife is a lawyer for the Bank of Nicaragua.

Family No. 6 — **The Nunez Tellez Tribe.** Carlos is on the junta and president of the State Council. Filiberto is vice-minister of construction. Rene is secretary of the Sandinista Party. Daughter Milena supervises the education department.

This is the bunch that lied to the people of Nicaragua, promising them equal shares of power and prosperity. Instead, they have taken it all for themselves, as Marxists always do, and the people are left holding the bag. . .an empty bag of promises. They are now worse off than ever.

COMMANDER ZERO

While speaking in Costa Rica in 1983, I was able to make contact with one of the chief advisors to the President of that country — President Monge. In fact, I had an invitation to visit with the Costa Rican President just before leaving Costa Rica, but it was postponed after an early morning death of the President's closest friend. To say the least, I shall look forward to meeting this Christian, anti-Communist leader of Costa Rica, one of the few democracies in Central and South America.

Costa Rica has a leftist country on its southern flanks. . Panama. . .and a Communist country on its northern flanks. . .Nicaragua. Therefore, it is sandwiched between two Communist countries, but Costa Rica has long been known for its democratic form of government and its religious freedom, as well as its free enterprise economic principles. However, the country is without an Army which, in my opinion, could lead to its downfall. In my personal conferences with leaders of the Costa Rican government, I suggested that they consider getting America's support and organizing a national army. How else can they defend their borders from Communist terrorists who are constantly coming into Costa Rica to do their dirty work from Panama, El Salvador and Nicaragua. The only official law enforcement in the country at the present is the Police Department. The nation is also plagued with thieves and pickpockets that infiltrate the country from Colombia.

However, you must realize that the tradition of Costa Rica is a democracy with a pacifist outlook. Like Switzerland, they would like to be a neutral country, never taking sides in any international conflict. But in today's world, when Communism is slowly, but surely taking over the entire free world in order to build the **World Government of the Anti-Christ**. Costa Rica's non-alignment policy might be its downfall. In fact, the new President has suggested that he might be friendly to the concept of America building a military base in the northern part of the country that is close to communist Nicaragua. Surely, an American military base in Costa Rica would discourage a Sandinista invasion of the country or a Panamanian invasion of the country.

One of the weeks that we were there, the Communist terrorists from El Salvador, slipped into the capitol city of San Jose and killed a Japanese industrialist who was active in Japanese investments in Costa Rica and living there. So, things are not 100% peaceful in Costa Rica. There are more and more outbreaks of terrorist activities, but they are being held — as much as possible — at a minimum by the democratic government there.

Newsweek's Big Story On CIA

Just a few days after my wife Betty and I arrived in Costa Rica, *Newsweek* magazine in the United States had printed in its November 8, 1982 edition a cover story entitled "**An Exclusive Report. . .America's Secret War. . .Target: Nicaragua.**" Beginning on page 42 of this particular issue, the story alleged that America had vested interest in Central America besides our desire to keep El Salvador from going Communist. . .that it would be best for America, according to the Reagan Administration, if the Sandinista Government of Nicaragua could be over-thrown by the anti-Communist guerrillas. I agree.

Now, there are two groups of anti-Communist guerrillas that are attempting to overthrow the Communist dictatorship in Nicaragua: 1. The military men who formerly served in President Somoza's Army and are now training anti-Communist guerrillas in a neighboring country to Nicaragua. . .Honduras. 2. The other group of anti-Communist guerrillas are being trained in Costa Rica and are lead by Commander Zero.

After reading the *Newsweek* article, I was determined to meet Commander Zero personally if it was humanly possible. I asked my friend who was the advisor to the President of Costa Rica, if he could arrange a meeting for me with the "legendary Commander Zero," and it was done, for which I am grateful.

Commander Zero, whose true name is Eden Pastora, was a national hero in Nicaragua prior to his resigning from the Sandinista Communist Government in July of 1981. According to my personal conversation with Commander Zero, America's CIA urged this man to overthrow the Communist dictatorship in his homeland of Nicaragua and install a democratic government similar to the one in Costa Rica. The CIA apparently wanted Commander Zero to go to Honduras where there are close to fifty CIA personnel active in supporting anti-Communist efforts from their Honduras base inside Nicaragua. Commander Zero would not accept this responsibility in Honduras, although he would have had no financial problems in either raising or training an anti-Communist Army in Honduras, made up of Nicaraguan refugees, because the CIA would have financed it. He preferred to "go it alone" in Costa Rica.

How We Got There

In my visit, Commander Zero told me of his political dreams and ideas for a future Nicaragua. He started out by telling me that he was opposed to Somoza, the late dictator, because of one thing, Somoza had killed his father who had been a champion of democracy and freedom in Nicaragua. He said, "Somoza representated torture, persecution and corruption. My father was assassinated by Somoza." I asked him about Somoza's own father who was alledgedly a friend of the United States — he answered me as one might expect that he would by saying, "Somoza's father was a robber, gangster and a thief, but he was more intelligent than his son. He ruled our country for 45 years." In answer to the question, "Why did the U.S. seem to like Somoza?" Commander Zero said, "When the United States likes a person, they love him regardless of what he does wrong. Now America paid for that mistake of loving Somoza in spite of his dictatorship by losing Nicaragua to the Communists. The people of the United States are noble, they love peace and they are moved by compassion towards people who are suffering or who are involved . in calamity." He furthermore said, "I love the Americans and I enjoy every visit with them."

I asked him which is worse — Nicaragua today under Communism or Nicaragua under Somoza. Naturally, it was hard for the man who stormed Somoza's palace and brought down the government in the capitol of Nicaragua to say that it was better under Somoza. He did say this: "In some instances, it is worse today under the Communists. Economically, the country has been ruined by Communism. Under Somoza we exported $900 million worth of goods and now we only export $400 million. Under Somoza we had political terror, but under Communism we have a police ordained terrorism."

Zero Relates His Inside Story

I asked him at what time did he know that the revolution was Communist and he answered, "We won in July and by September I knew, because we didn't condemn Russia's invasion of Afghanistan. We also violated our non-alignment promises to the Nicaraguan people. We had promised not to be pro-Russian or pro-American. Beyond a shadow of a doubt, I know that we were allied with Moscow. We had been betrayed and the one man who betrayed our revolution to bring democracy to our country was Umberto Ortega who was the brother to Daniel Ortega. He was always the leader. He was the one who was getting the money from the Russians and the rest of us didn't know it."

Then, this legendary and disillusioned patriot told me how 40,000 to 50,000 people were killed during the revolution to obtain freedom for Nicaragua, taking time to dwell on the fact that most of them were innocent people.

He talked of the priest who is the present Minister of defense and who is now an out-and-out Communist, in spite of being a Roman Catholic priest. He said of him, "He was always with Somoza when he was alive. Now, he is with the Communists. He is a political opportunist. His name is Meguel D'Scotto. He wants to be the leader. He would like to over-power the nine Communist Generals that run the government and be the leader. There are nine in power. They will not fight each other. They are Stalinists. They are not philosophical Marxists. They are Stalinists. Anybody with eyes knows that they are not Marxists serving some cause — they are just brutal Stalinists killing and torturing."

Referring to Costa Rica, his host country, he said: "Now, Costa Rica is in danger. Democracy here is in danger and the danger comes from the outside — from Nicaragua. I want to lead a secret army in Nicaragua. I lack support because the Communists in charge of the Nicaraguan government say that I represent the Right Wing, while some of the leaders in favor of democracy in Nicaragua believe that I have sold out to the Left Wing because I was with the other nine in the Sandinista Revolution."

He would keep saying to me, "Help us. Tell President Reagan to help democracy in our courtry — to help those of us who still fight for freedom. We once fought for freedom and we are still fighting for freedom. We are the ones who can bring peace to Nicaragua. Talk to your leaders so that they will not help finance the Sandinistas or the Somoza forces — for the love of peace, for the love of your fellowman."

During the interview, I asked Commander Zero if he had read the November 8 *Newsweek* magazine and he had. I quoted a statement that had been allegedly made by one of his own men who said that if Commander Zero ever took CIA support in order to free Nicaragua that he would "**Kill him myself.**"

Let us remember that President Carter aided the Communist Revolution in Nicaragua by sending millions and millions of dollars and economic assistance to the Communist Revolution. Prior to his leaving the White House, the President sent his own wife to Nicaragua to make a personal promise on behalf of her husband that the U.S. would continue to support the Red Sandinistas. We had a president then who was naive about the internal threat of Communism and naive about the international threat of Communism and yet, keep the record straight — this same President had the courage to pull America out of the international Olympics in Moscow because Russia invaded Afghanistan. We must all applaud that act. Furthermore, President Carter later seemed to more and more be changing his misguided views of Communism. However, he had a blind spot when it came to the Communist Revolution in Nicaragua. He was not willing to admit that the government of Panama was a Communist Government and he had given the Panama Canal to this Communist enemy. He was not willing to admit that the communist Sandinistas in Nicaragua would try to turn all of Central America against the United States.

Concerning The CIA In Honduras

Personally, in spite of the liberal politicians and news media opposing CIA agents training anti-Communist guerrillas in Central America, I am all for it. I support President Reagan's concern over the Communist presence in Nicaragua.

I was tremendously impressed with Commander Zero. Even though I don't want to offend this man who was so kind and considerate of me while I was his guest, I must say that on the surface he seems to lack a deep knowledge of the Communist conspiracy. Although I feel certain that he is neither Communist nor pro-Communist, like a great deal of our fellow Americans, he does not fully understand the Communist threat or the Communist cause. He is anti-Communist. He knows that Communists betrayed the revolution that he lead to bring Nicaragua into the Democratic camp. He wants nothing to do with Russia or any other Communist country, and yet he speaks of non-alignment. This is Third World talk. It is the kind of talk that gets you nowhere. **You must either be "for" or "against" Communism.** You cannot be for Democracy and not be against Communism.

I asked him at one point if he had any money. How did he feed his troops inside of Nicaragua who were fighting the Civil War to overthrow the government. He pulled out a briefcase and showed me $100,000 in $100 U.S. currency and then he showed me $20,000 in Nicaraguan money. That was all of the money that he had. He was financing an army — moreover, he was financing a revolution with less than $120,000. That proves that he is a man of idealism. Naturally, he couldn't get any support from Russia because Russia is quite well pleased with the nine Communists who run the Sandinistan

Government of Nicaragua. But, he turned down whatever support that he could have received from the CIA because he could not conscientiously work with the former Somoza aides — since some of them assassinated his father.

Debunking The Kissinger Report

In the last few years, both myself and Bill Sampson, editor of our *Christian Crusade* Newspaper, have spent more time in Central America than the so-called "Kissinger Commission" which came out with a report in 1984 recommending the spending of $8 billion on combined military and economic aid in the area, so we feel as well qualified as anyone else to comment on the report that drew a lot of praise from the national news media, which meant that liberals were pretty pleased with whatever was being praised.

We believe that American economic and military aid is necessary for survival of freedom in Central America and possibly the entire Western Hemisphere, but we challenge the way in which the Kissinger Report recommends it be spent.

The trouble with the Kissinger Commission report is that its spending plan almost ignores the shooting war going on in Central America. It wants to put the cart of economic development ahead or alongside the horse of military victory that is necessary for peace.

In other words, the Kissinger Commission report makes the same mistake that has been made in Central America since the war there began with the Marxist revolution that overthrew the Somoza government in Nicaragua. That mistake is that you can have economic development in the midst of a war. You can't.

That's the kind of mistake President Lyndon Johnson made in trying to fight the war in Vietnam while at the same time spending billions on the so-called "Great Society" of social welfare programs.

It is the basic economic mistake that dates back centuries. You can't have both guns (big military expenditures) and butter (consumer goods expenditures) in abundance at the same time or else you will go broke. That's what happened to America in the 1960s and we are still living with the mad paper money inflation which began then.

Now along comes the Kissinger Commission making the same mistake, urging that President Reagan and the Congress spend money in Central America on both economic development and military assistance while a war is going on.

Having observed the war in El Salvador first hand and

148

having traveled Central America looking at economic conditions and talking to people about life there, I contend that the war must be won first before any economic development can be effective.

By "the war," I mean the communist revolution initiated, supplied and maintained by the Soviet Union and its stooge Cuba. Until the communists are defeated and driven out of Central America, no amount of economic aid there will do any good.

There are too many ignorant people in positions of power in Washington who simply refuse to understand or admit to themselves that the communists are the cause of the war in Central America. Certainly the region has economic problems but they cannot be solved until there is peace. There cannot be peace until the communists are defeated and driven out.

To spend $8 billion over the next five years in Central America as the Kissinger Commission suggests is foolish and doomed to failure unless the military issue there — the war — is resolved first by victory over the communists. Such a victory likely would cost more than the $8 billion but to pour $8 billion into Central America as it is now will be like pouring a bucket of water onto the Sahara Desert and expecting a garden to bloom. It won't happen.

The United States already is running a national budget deficit of nearly $200 billion a year which is being added onto a total national debt of well over $1 trillion. Who is going to pay for this extra $8 billion? Guess who? The already overburdened American taxpayer who is still financing the deficit spending of the New Deal, the New Frontier, the Great Society, the Vietnam War and the largest social welfare and defense programs in history.

Before we spend $8 billion on Central America, there must be a change of thinking and priorities in this country, in Washington and among the people. That's not likely to happen if I know anything about the federal government and national politics and I think I do.

Here is what none of the politicians want to stand up and say right now:

1. Cut government spending to the bone until the budget is balanced and we quit running a deficit, no matter whose ox is gored or special interest is hurt. To try to balance the budget with a tax increase instead of spending cuts is doing nothing more than adding to the monstrous national debt because the additional paper money that would have to be used to pay taxes already is over-valued and is worth practically nothing.

149

Printing up more of it for a tax increase to balance the budget is not only inflationary but in reality increases the debt instead of paying if off because of the worthless paper money premise upon which the government operates under virtual control of the privately-owned controller of the currency, the Federal Reserve.

Until our own financial house is in order it is foolhardy to spend $8 billion in Central America or anywhere else in the world for an illusionary pursuit of peace or prosperity.

2. Face the hard facts about Central America and the communist war going on if peace is truly wanted there. The United States is going to have to have either get in or get out. The halfway measures we have been using are not going to succeed. If we get in, it will mean sending combat forces to the region. If we do that, we should go in to win and not fight in a half-hearted, hands-tied war like Korea or Vietnam. If we go in, we should go in to win quickly and decisively in an operation like Grenada. Otherwise, stay out and let the communists have it. If the communists take Central America, they will push on militarily into Mexico, already rotten to the core and controlled by communist bureaucrats. That would put militant communism on the Rio Grande, right behind a flood of an estimated 20 million refugees, fleeing into the United States.

3. The Kissinger Commission report is a phony compromise and doomed to failure because Kissinger and the commissioners did not have the courage to face up to the facts in Central America about the true nature of communism. The sheer ruthlessness of communism in Central America is being opposed by the sheer ruthlessness of privately-financed "death squads" there that make it their business to kill communists and suspected communists. The "death squads" don't rely on justice anymore than the communists. It is a kill or be killed war and in war, human rights are meaningless. The commission's hand-wringing over human rights is an act of political hypocrisy when a war is going on. The commission is kidding itself and its readers into thinking that the war is somehow secondary and not going on.

4. The Kissinger Commission undermined itself with a plan to invite communists into the administration of the $8 billion aid program. The economic development program would be administered by an American chairman and "representatives" of all seven Central American nations including Marxist Nicaragua and Panama. The Nicaraguans would be invited on the condition that Nicaragua "agrees to internal reform." That's a laugh. That's like urging internal reform on Soviet Russia or Cuba or

Red China. It won't happen but what will happen is that enough leftist, liberal political and media pressure will be brought to bear on the powers behind the development administration that the communists will be allowed on the controlling body, reform or no reform. At the same time, failure to curb the "death squads" could get the El Salvador representative thrown off the panel. It would be like what happened when Red China got Free China thrown out of the United Nations.

The proposed "development organization" for Central America that would be set up to spend the $8 billion has been called by the liberal press "a Marshall Plan for Central America" but it is no such thing. Failure is built into it if communists are allowed on the governing board as the Kissinger Commission report suggests.

The plan proposes that most of the money be spent on such basic needs as food, education, health and construction of roads, ports, bridges and other "labor intensive" or — as I would say it — "make-work" projects.

This is throwing money down a rathole if military victory over communism is not achieved first.

To keep the communists from crossing the Rio Grande, we will have to fortify our southern border for the first time in history or else see to it that a military victory is won decisively over communism in Central America. Either way, it's going to cost far more than the $8 billion in the Kissinger Commission report but that's probably all the commission thought it could realistically and politically recommend at this time.

Drawing the line on communism in Central America is exactly what the much-criticized Alexander Haig said when he first took office as Secretary of State in 1981, only to be hooted out by the leftist, liberal national news media. Now the Kissinger Commission is saying the same thing Haig said, only without the conviction Haig had that military victory there is necessary before peace and prosperity can be achieved with economic aid.

We can't have it both ways. We have to decide whether or not Central America is really in our national interest, our vital interest. If it is, we should fight for it and win a decisive military victory over communism. If it isn't, we should abandon it to its communist fate. We can't buy it with foreign aid.

By abandoning Central America, we can postpone the decision until the communist tanks roll up to the Rio Grande, then we will be faced with the choice all over again only in a much worse strategic situation.

Maybe the time has come at last for America to learn the truth about communism; that it is serious about dominating the entire world including the United States of America.

The communists will not be satisfied with taking Central America anymore than they have been satisfied with taking over Russia or Cuba or Nicaragua or Red China or Zimbabwe or Angola or Eastern Europe or Southeast Asia or anyplace else they have seized.

The atheistic communists will not stop with just El Salvador or Central America or Mexico. They want it all, all the world. When Americans become convinced of that, this country will awake to the alarm Billy James Hargis and Christian Crusade have been sounding. They will realize that the fight is not just political but is the conflict between good and evil, between God and Satan.

The only real value I can see in the Kissinger Commission report is that if it is taken seriously it could touch off a national debate about the extent of the communist threat in this hemisphere and perhaps teach a few people the true meaning and goals of godless communism.

Nicaragua's Persecution of Christians

What I want to know is when is the World Court going to find communist Nicaragua guilty of persecuting Christians?

They were mighty quick to condemn the United States for mining Nicaraguan waters in a futile effort to stop Soviet arms shipments into Nicaragua for transport to the communist invaders of El Salvador. But the World Court and the international press have been very quiet about Nicaragua's lid on religious freedom.

Nicaragua has been communist for years, now, and one of the first things communist governments do is take over the church, stamp out free religion, control the church for the benefit of the state. That's the way it works with the Russian Orthodox Church in the Soviet Union and the much publicized Protestant churches there . . . and that's the way it works in Nicaragua.

Not too long ago the *Christian Crusade Newspaper* reported the story of a young fundamentalist Christian who was fasely arrested by the Nicaraguan communist government, beaten, tortured, and had his ears cut off. It hasn't stopped there.

The Catholic Church in Nicaragua, has been persecuted, certainly, with priests arrested, churches closed and even the Pope insulted and his pastoral letter to Nicaraguans censored by the communist government there.

But there has been a lot of unpublicized persecution of Protestant minorities in Nicaragua, too. The Nicaraguan Marxists accuse the Protestants of being "anti-revolutionary" because they believe in Christ, calls them fanatics and superstitious people and agents of American imperialism.

Some 20 Protestant churches in the capital of Managua were seized by what the Nicaraguan communist government called "**divine mobs**" and their properties confiscated. The churches have been instructed that their properties will be returned only upon the promise that they do not criticize the government. How can a true Christian minister not criticize godless, Satanic, communism that is dedicated to the destruction of Christianity?

I praise God for the courage of those persecuted Christians in communist Nicaragua who have been brave enough to stand up and tell the people the truth about godless communism and explain to them that you cannot be both a Christian and a communist, as the Nicaraguan (and Soviet) government would have people believe. I pray that the ministers in the United States will soon begin telling their congregations the same thing, before it is too late. It is their duty! It is their duty as Christians! Christ's church is threatened by Satan at the very doorstep of this country and we have ministers preaching the prosperity gospel, appealing to man's base instincts for covetousness, when they should be preaching that there is not going to be **any prosperity for anyone** if communism takes over America.

The communist government of Nicaragua has been persecuting the Protestant Indians of that nation's isolated Atlantic coast — the Miskitos, Sumas and Ramas. Their missionaries and ministers were told to submit all sermons to the state for approval — a common practice throughout Nicaragua. When they refused, in one village, armed troops moved in, herded the villagers into the church, then took several women out and raped them, then killed them, then machine-gunned the men in the church. Did you see the headlines? No, this massacre was largely ignored by the international press and completely ignored by the United Nations and most so-called "Human Rights" organizations. Martial law has been declared in dozens of indian villages. People are being summarily executed without trial for the least infractions, including worship.

The Organization of American States has been informed of all this by indian exiles and has printed dozens of press releases, few of which ever are considered newsworthy by the big television networks and other major news media.

The overwhelming evidence of widespread persecution of Christian churches in Nicaragua reveals once again the **Satanic and sadistic nature** of communism and its total war on freedom of religion.

Chapter 8

CUBA: CORE OF THE CANCER

Fidel Castro's Communist Cuba is not only the largest armed threat to American security in the Western Hemisphere, he and his Marxist country are also the hemisphere's biggest drug pushers.

Cuba is using the drug business to finance communist revolution in Latin America.

Selected drug traffickers, operating under special favor from Castro, are allowed to use Cuban waters as a haven from the U.S. Coast Guard while trans-shipping narcotics to the United States from Colombia. Castro gets as much as $500,000 per shipment for such favors and uses much of the money to buy arms from the Soviets and from Eastern European communist bloc countries and then the drug smugglers secretly ferry them to Red guerrillas in Central America on their return trips for more drugs.

The authority for this drug traffic is Frank V. Monasero, assistant administrator of the U.S. Drug Enforcement Administration. He says there is "evidence of a considerable amount of drug trafficking that transits through Cuba by both air and water. The smugglers sometimes use Cuban government facilities. If the Cuban government wanted to cease that activity, it could put a stop to it."

Much of the Cuban drug trafficking was exposed in a 1983 criminal trial in Miami when four Cuban government officials were among several people charged with conspiring to permit Cuba to be used as a loading station for U.S.-bound drug vessels. Six people were convicted, including a former Cuban ambassador to Colombia and a vice admiral who belonged to the Cuban Communist Party's Central Committee. Both failed to appear at the trial and since then have been considered fugitives from justices by the U.S. Justice Department.

A key figure in the Cuba-Colombia arms and drug smuggling racket is Jaime Guillot-Lara, a Colombian national who fled to Mexico to avoid U.S. warrants and extradition papers that were to be served on him in Colombia. Mexican authorities, sympathetic to communism, refused a U.S. government request to extradite Guillot-Lara and his whereabouts have not been known since then.

The U.S. government estimates his 15-member gang has shipped up to 5 million pounds of marijuana, 160 pounds of cocaine and 50 million Quaaludes into the United States between 1977 and 1985.

Under Cuban sponsorship and with Castro's approval, Guillot-Lara, working with Cuba's main terrorist group known as M-19, used some of the drug income received in Florida to purchase Uzi submachine guns, AR-15 rifles and other weapons and ammunition from an illegal Miami arms dealer. His ship, the Zar de Honduras, is well-known in the Gulf of Mexico and the Caribbean. It is known that it received a major arms shipment from a mysterious (believed to be communist) ship off the coast of Panama and trans-shipped them to Nicaragua for forwarding to Red terrorists and guerrillas in El Salvador. The shipment included 550 FAL rifles worth about $500 apeace and nearly one million cartridges.

Guillot-Lara's gang, plus certain members of Cuba's M-19 hand-picked by Castro, plus Colombian communists tax Colombian drug growers in return for "protection." They also buy the growers' crops and provide "protection" for drug-smuggling air strips and secret sea ports from Colombian government authorities, many of whom are believed to be bribed anyway.

The Colombian government officially broke diplomatic ties with Cuba in 1981 but the drug traffic continues. Honest Colombian officials are engaged in a shooting war with the M-19 Cubans and communist guerrillas in the country. More than 100 Reds once seized and temporarily occupied the town of Florencia, capital of Caqueta province. They were eventually driven away by Colombian army units but not until they had looted many businesses and freed 125 prisoners from the jail, most of them subversives who fled with the Reds into the Colombian jungles and mountains.

The Cuba-Colombia "deal" was made in a series of meetings

in 1979-1980 at the Bogota Hilton Hotel attended by Guillot-Lara, Colombian Ambassador Revelo, Cuba's minister-counselor to Colombia, Gonzalo Bassols, and a Colombian lawyer and admitted drug dealer identified as Juan (Johnny) Crump. They agreed that Guillot-Lara'ss drug boats, flying a Panamania flag and using the code name "Viviana," would be assured safe passage through Cuban waters and, implicitly, use of Cuban beaches or small fishing ports for trans-shipment of drugs, with Castro's government getting its cut on every shipment.

A trawler with the name "Viviana" was seized by the U.S. Coast Guard off the North Carolina coast after a search turned up 40,000 pounds of marijuana with an estimated value of $16 million.

A Defense Department intelligence report says the Cuban government has become so bold in the drug traffic as to rent a merchant ship from a Panamanian owner for $24,000 a month to move narcotics north from Colombia to a small island off Cuba's southern coast for trans-shipment to Florida. U.S. records quote a Cuban vice-admiral as saying: "We are going to fill Miami completely with drugs." The records also quote Guillot-Lara as having said: "I have enough money to do any type of business with Cuba."

Despite all this evidence, several members of the U.S. Congress continue to push for diplomatic recognition of Castro's Cuba, or, at least, to open an official "dialogue" with the Red dictator, even with the knowledge that Castro is the No. 1 drug trafficker in the Western Hemisphere. This should be remembered whenever some liberal Congressman makes a speech in favor of restoring diplomatic relations with the Cuban gangster. There is *irrefutable evidence* that Castro's navy has been used to transport at least 5 million illegal drug tablets and 1,000 pounds of marijuana to Florida. Communist drug traffickers are bringing a big part of the $80 billion a year illegal drug smuggling business into the United States. They make money and they *drug American youth.* No, it's not time for any diplomatic recognition of Castro the drug runner.

Castro's communist Cuba is the hemispheric core of the cancer of communism now starting to encircle America. It has become a definite and direct military threat to the security of the United States and it is the headquarters of communist revolution in this hemisphere.

Cuba's military strength has increased and its military capabilities have improved dramatically over the last five years, far in excess of any actual or imaginary defensive needs.

Cuba's armed forces include an army of more than 225,000, a navy of 11,000 and an air force of 16,000. These figures do not include additional hundreds of thousands of paramilitary forces which in many cases are better trained and better equipped than the regular armed forces of other Caribbean countries.

Cuba has more than 2.3 per cent of its population in the regular armed forces and one of every 20 Cubans participates in some kind of "security mission." By comparison, Mexico, with seven times Cuba's population, has defense forces half the size of Cuba and less than two-tenths of one per cent of its people in the armed forces. Brazil, the largest Latin American country, has about the same percentage as Mexico. The United States has less than one per cent of our people in the armed forces.

Castro has a military force 10 to 20 times larger on a per capita basis than any of the other major nations in this hemisphere.

The Cubans have more than 200 MIG fighter planes supplied by the Soviet Union, 650 tanks, 90 helicopters, 2 Foxtrot-style attack submarines, 1 Koni-class frigate and about 50 torpedo and missile attack boats.

All this military strength is under the direction of the Soviet Union. The Soviets have a military brigade of 3,000 men stationed in Havana. There are an additional 8,000 Soviet civilian advisors in Cuba. Another 2,000 Soviet military advisers provide technical advice and support for such sophisticated weapons as the MIGS, surface-to-air missiles and the submarines. The Soviets also maintain a major intelligence collection facility near Havana which monitors U.S. civil and military communications.

This massive Soviet-Cuban military might and intelligence center sits astride critical sea lanes of communication in the Caribbean. In peacetime, 44 per cent of all our foreign trade shipping tonnage and 45 per cent of the crude oil to the United States passes through the Caribbean Sea. In the event of war, fully half of the North Atlantic Treaty Alliance's supplies are scheduled to transit by sea from Gulf ports through the Florida straits and onward to Europe.

The security of maritime operations in the Caribbean is critical to the security of the Atlantic Alliance and the defense of Western Europe.

The increased presence of Soviet military and naval strength in Cuba poses a grave threat to the Atlantic Alliance lifeline. In 1970, Soviet naval vessels spent about 200 ship days in the

South Atlantic. In 1980, this number had increased 13-fold to 2,600 ship days. Given the present strength and disposition of the U.S. Navy, the sea lanes of communication in the South Atlantic and the Caribbean are far more vulnerable today than they were in the days of the Cuban missile crisis.

The Soviet Union has armed Cuba to the teeth. The total value of Soviet arms shipments to Cuba since 1960 is $2.5 billion. Since Cuban intervention in Angola, the average yearly totals have doubled. In 1981, Cuba received 63,000 metric tons of arms from the Soviet Union, the highest yearly total since the massive buildup in the missile crisis year of 1962.

Beginning with its support of the Sandinista revolution in Nicaragua in 1978, Cuba has increased its support for communist revolution in Latin America in very dramatic ways. Cuba is not only a training base for communist revolutionaries and terrorists, but Castro's agents are active in the field throughout the region. For example, there were more than 1,500 Cuban military personnel in Nicaragua at the outset of 1982. There were another 4,300 non-military Cuban personnel in that country, many to indoctrinate the new communist education system with communist theory based on the teachings of Marx and Lenin. Cuba supplies weapons to Red revolutionaries throughout the hemisphere both directly and as a conduit from the Soviet bloc, Libya, Algeria and Iraq. Cuba also supplies a safe-haven for guerrilla personnel, a transit point for military training for them in the Soviet Union, and is a clearing house for money to rebel forces in Latin America.

Cuba has become the greatest threat to freedom and is the "crown colony of Soviet imperialism," according to Dr. Fred Ilke, Undersecretary of Defense for Policy.

Unlike the ill-fated revolutionary expedition of Che Guevara into Bolivia and elsewhere during the early 1960s, Cuban subversion today is backed up by an extensive secret intelligence and training apparatus, modern military armaments from the Soviet bloc and personnel recruited from countries targeted for revolution, and by a large, effective and sophisticated propaganda network.

Castro's plan, and it is working, is to supply weapons, training and ideological support for violent revolutionary groups — sometimes several in the same country — then coerce them to unite under his leadership by threatening to cut them off and isolate them from a united organization. This is the way unification was achieved among disparate groups in El Salvador. The various minor leaders are usually flown to

Managua, Nicaragua, to sign a unification pact with each other under supervision of a Castro agent, and then flown to Havana to meet the great man himself, Castro, who adds the pact to a portfolio of such agreements he is collecting from revolutionaries in every Latin American country.

Castro tried diplomacy unsuccessfully in the 1970s. His attempt to be officially recognized as the leader of the "Third World" or so-called non-aligned countries failed. His Guevara-inspired attempts to export revolution with his own hand-picked men failed in the 1960s. So at the beginning of the 1980s, Castro made a public announcement of a new policy toward revolution.

In his July 26, 1980, speech, Castro declared that the experience of Guatemala, El Salvador, Chile and Bolivia taught him that there is no other way than revolution, that there is no other "formula" as he called it, than "revolutionary armed struggle."

Castro's statement was simply a public attempt to justify what he and his agents have been doing secretly since 1978, namely, stepping up support for armed revolution in neighboring countries.

After Guevara's fatal fiasco in 1967, when neither the peasantry nor the Bolivian Communist Party supported him, Castro moved even closer to the Soviet Union. He endorsed the 1968 Soviet invasion of Czechoslovakia. In the mid-1970s, he invaded several African countries to assist Soviet foreign policy goals there. Moscow could use the Cubans to intervene in Africa where it could not diplomatically use its own troops. Soviet Russia increased its aid to Cuba to $3 billion annually to finance such foreign adventures by Castro. The Soviets directed Castro to use his African tactics in Latin America, only employing native guerrillas enlisted into communism instead of using Cuban troops directly. Cuba also became the arms broker for communist guerrillas in the region.

Cuba has sold its economic and military soul to the Soviets who call the shots for Cuban foreign policy. By intervening in behalf of armed struggle in Latin America, Cuba injects powerful East-West or U.S.-Soviet dimensions into what would otherwise be local conflicts. This is a major reason why El Salvador has been such a knotty problem for the United States and the government it has supported there.

Kicking the communists out of El Salvador is to kick Cuba and Soviet Russia in the teeth. Washington has not had the guts to do that yet for fear of retaliation and reluctance to start World War III on a larger global scale.

By using Cuba as its military front in the Western Hemisphere, Moscow can maintain a low diplomatic profile and cultivate state-to-state relationships and economic ties with major countries like Brazil and Argentina.

In turn, Cuba is careful not to undercut the Soviets where they have established such valuable relations. In Peru, for example, Cuba has restrained its revolutionary methods so as not to jeopardize the status of some 300 Soviet officials in that country. It wouldn't be worth risking the arms supplies and economic subsidy received from Russia.

Cuba made tremendous strides in the propaganda field. Presna Latina, the press agency of Castro's government, and Radio Havana, in close coordination with the Soviet news agency TASS and Radio Moscow, deliberately publish and broadcast misinformation to distort news reports throughout Latin America, especially in places where Cuba's covert revolutionary activity is more intense, such as El Salvador.

Pandering to widespread illiteracy in Latin America, Cuba concentrates on radio broadcasts which require no particular education to hear and understand. Radio Havana transmits more than 350 program hours in eight languages to all of Latin America. In addition, Cuba broadcasts "La Voz de Cuba" in Spanish each night over a network of high-powered transmitters located throughout Cuba. The propaganda is broadcast over separate transmitters in Spanish, English, French and Creole (for Haiti).

These communist broadcasts are filled with fraud and lies but the listeners don't know that. The broadcasts are designed to do one thing: promote communism. And if promoting communism means attacking the United States, disparaging free economies, and criticizing Christ and His church, then the unscrupulous communist broadcasters do it. On the other hand, the American government's "Voice of America" broadcasts into the region are not allowed to engage in Christian preaching or even anti-communist programming because of political State Department restrictions on program content. It is little wonder the communists are winning the propaganda battle.

Following is a series of reports in a "nutshell" on how Cuba has involved itself in various Latin American countries. This is not intended to be a comprehensive history of the countries but an illustration of proven and provable Cuban communist intervention and invasion in Latin America:

Nicaragua
The communist revolution against Somoza didn't begin to

jell until early 1978 when Armando Ulises Estrada began making many secret trips between Havana and Nicaragua. Estrada was a high ranking official of what Castro calls his "America Department," which is his agency for international subversion. Estrada unified three major communist revolutionary factions that had been carrying on a disorganized "armed struggle" against Somoza. Their unification was announced in public at the 11th World Youth Festival in Havana in July, 1978. By the end of 1978, the revolutionaries had been properly trained and armed by Cuban advisors stationed in Costa Rica.

In early 1979, Cuba organized, armed and transported to Nicaraga a so-called "international brigade" of guerrillas from several Central and South American extremist groups, many of them experienced terrorists. They fought on the side of the Sandinistas in Nicaragua so effectively that they became a divisive force themselves and Castro held a personal audience in Havana with all the leaders of the revolutionary forces in Nicaragua to hammer out a renewed unity pact. During the "final offensive" against Somoza in mid-1979, many Cuban military advisors were wounded in combat and evacuated to Cuba via Panama.

The communist victory in Nicaragua secured a base on the mainland for a major buildup of Red military forces as well as a convenient trans-shipment point for men and equipment to supply additional revolutions in the rest of Central America, especially El Salvador and Guatemala, with Honduras, Costa Rica and Belize expected to be secondary targets likely to fall with less effort.

The communists quickly took advantage of the Nicaragua position to make a huge military buildup there. The Central Intelligence Agency exposed this prime launching pad for communist subversion throughout the rest of Central America at a special press conference in Washington on March 9, 1982. Admiral Bobby Inman, then deputy director of the CIA, used aerial photographs to show major improvements at four airfields so military jets can be accommodated, Soviet-style barracks and training areas, sites for military equipment storage and traffic indicating vast military activity in Nicaragua. The CIA said Nicaragua has 70,000 men in the army, militia and reserves and has been receiving Soviet tanks and other weaponry considered to be offensive weapons rather than defensive.

The Nicaraguans denied they were helping in El Salvador and said the buildup was justified because they feared an American invasion.

The liberals in Congress were not convinced by the CIA evidence. One Congressman, Rep. Michael Barnes of Maryland, chairman of the House Inter-American Affairs Subcommittee, asked: *"What are we trying to do? It is almost as if the administration wants a war in Central America."*

That kind of rhetoric is head-in-the-sand thinking. How can any intelligent reasoning, in the face of vast evidence, convince anyone, much less a national leader such as Rep. Barnes, that it is United States wanting war in Central America? The war is already going on there, directed from Moscow, orchestrated by Cuba, and carried on by dedicated communists who have been indoctrinated and trained politically in Marxism and Leninism, and armed by the Soviet Union and its allies.

Today some 5,000 Cuban advisors, teachers and medical personnel work at all levels of the communist government ruling Nicaragua. More than 1,500 of them are strictly military, providing military training, combat instruction and both intelligence and counter-intelligence leadership for the growing Nicaraguan army. Between October 1980 and February 1981, Nicaragua was the staging site for a massive Cuban-directed flow of arms to communist guerrillas in El Salvador and for training and transportation of guerrillas into Guatemala.

Following the July, 1979, victory of the Sandinistas in Nicaragua, Armando Estrada was appointed Castro's ambassador to Jamaica and in 1982 was Cuba's ambassador to South Yemen.

El Salvador

The same strategy of unification of various communist revolutionary groups has been used to unite the communist armed forces in El Salvador. Following the battlefield defeat of the communists during their "final offensive" of January, 1981, Cuba has reorganized and rearmed the guerrillas, this time training them in battalion sized units of 250 to 500 men so they will be able to mount major military campaigns instead of mere hit-and-run terrorist tactics. They have been receiving anywhere from three to seven months military training in Nicaragua, and some have been sent to Palestinian Liberation Organization camps for training in the Middle East. A few have been trained as "officers" in Soviet Russia.

Without Cuban military training and equipment supplied by the Soviet Union and its bloc of allies, the El Salvador "revolution" would already be over. Cuba is the hemispheric base for communist revolution and Nicaragua is the Central

America staging ground for it. The communist trouble in El Salvador will continue so long as the Soviet-Cuba-Nicaragua Axis supplies the men and training to fuel it or until there is a change in American policy about blockading the flow of communist men and arms into Central America from Cuba or Russia or both.

Guatemala

The military coup that took over Guatemala in early 1982 was in direct response to the Cuban-supported communist revolution threatening to topple a weak and indecisive government there that could not make up its mind or policy whether to resist communism.

Guatemala's communist factions had not been unified by Castro as they had been in Nicaragua and El Salvador but they were on the verge of it when the coup happened. The terrorists in Guatemala had stepped up their violent actions in an effort to provoke "repression" or, in other words, resistance, for propaganda purposes in an effort to destablize the government. The coup thwarted that strategy for the time.

In 1981, arms shipped from Cuba to Nicaragua were smuggled to Guatemala, passing overland through Honduras. The guerilla arsenal in Guatemala includes 50 millimeter mortars, submachine guns, rocket launchers and other weapons. Captured M-16 rifles have been traced through records in the United States to Vietnam, where they had been abandoned when the U.S. forces left there. The M-16s have been shipped around the world to help arm communist forces in this hemisphere.

Documents and prisoners captured by Guatemalan defense forces attest to the fact that many of the communist guerrillas operating in the country were trained in Cuba as early as 1980. They received both urban and rural guerrilla warfare training in the use of explosives and firearms. They had traveled in some cases by public bus through Costa Rica to Panama, where they were issued Panamanian passports and flown to Cuba for training.

A joint bulletin issued by certain communist guerrilla groups in January, 1981, announced that Guatemalan guerrillas have collaborated with Salvadoran guerrillas and that the Salvadorans have provided the Guatemalans with a small quantity of arms. The significance of this announcement is that the guerrillas are in fact international communists willing to fight anywhere and not just native rebels demanding "justice" from an "oppressive" local government, as communist propaganda would have us believe.

Costa Rica

Costa Rica has been deeply involved in Cuba's Central America intrigues since the Nicaraguan revolution. A Costa Rican government investigation has revealed that at least one million pounds of arms moved from Cuba through Costa Rica into Nicaragua during the fighting there. It determined that there were at least 21 flights carrying war material between Cuba and Costa Rican airports in Llano Grande and Juan Santamaria during the Nicaraguan fighting. Costa Rican pilots who flew some of those missions testified they were often accompanied by Cuban advisor and directors.

The investigation revealed that when the communists won in Nicaragua, the flow of arms traffic through Costa Rica was then directed to El Salvador.

In May, 1981, Costa Rica broke diplomatic relations with Cuba over this continued clandestine arms traffic and expelled one Fernando Perez, among other Cuban consulate employees, who was identified as the chief coordinator of the Cuban military logistics program in Costa Rica.

While Costa Rica has a variety of communist and leftist splinter groups operating in the country, the one with the closest ties to Cuba is the Revolutionary Movement of the People, known as MRP. Costa Rican security police have raided communist meetings and seized documents clearly connecting them with the MRP, raids in which a quantity of arms and terrorist paraphernalia such as machine guns with silencers were confiscated. Several terrorists arrested in Costa Rica are known MRP members. The leader of the MRP has traveled many times to Cuba and Cuba has trained many other MRP members, organizers and secondary level leaders.

Honduras

Cuba enlisted and trained members of the Honduras Communist Party — known as PCH in the "international brigade" that fought in Nicaragua. After that war, many PCH international brigade veterans were selected for advanced training in Cuba.

Cuba has used Honduras mostly as a trans-shipment point for arms and men to El Salvador since the Nicaraguan fighting. But it has also begun to unite the various extremist groups in Honduras into one organization with the promise of arms and supplies, although this work has not yet reached the scale of that in El Salvador and Guatemala. In the typical pattern, Castro is increasing the political and military training of rebel bands with the obvious intent of using them eventually for revolution in Costa Rica or as part of a new and larger "international brigade" in El Salvador or Guatemela or wherever it might be needed, as decided by Castro, in the future.

Honduran authorities have in recent times begun to fight back against this communist military traffic and training in their country. Several so-called "safe houses" or communist meeting places have been raided and incriminating documents and notebooks verifying training in Cuba were confiscated along with caches of arms and communications equipment.

Inside Cuba

In the military aspect of what has been happening in the Caribbean and Central America, Cuba can only be viewed as a gigantic aircraft carrier of the Soviet Union anchored at the backyard of the United States.

From one end of the island to another Castro has more than 100 guerrilla training schools for international communist revolutionaries. It is a communist Trojan Horse with military men and equipment bursting its seams. It is a Soviet arsenal overloaded with men, missiles, planes, guns and ships.

Three Cuban airfields have been turned into military bases housing six different styles of Soviet MIG fighter planes piloted by Russians. The giant Tupoler TU-95 "Bear" planes armed with air-to-surface nuclear missiles with a range of 400 miles are frequent visitors to Cuba. All these aircraft fly tantalizingly close to U.S. shores on intelligence-gathering, reconnaisance and training missions. They also keep track of U.S. naval movements throughout the region.

The Soviets have spent $25 million establishing a huge naval base at Cienfuegos to neutralize the American naval base at Guantanamo. In September of 1970, during a "mini-crisis" between Washington and Moscow, the Soviets promised to dismantle the base but like most of their other promises, they didn't keep it. Reports from both the internal resistance in Cuba and the CIA are that the base is in full operation in the 1980s.

Cuba is the umbilical cord of all the subversion, agitation, unrest, revolution and terrorism in the Americas and has been since Castro established it as a base in the Western Hemisphere for the international communist movement in 1959. Castro has repeatedly pledged in public speeches and statements his support to the leftist guerrilla groups everywhere.

As early as 1959, shortly after Castro took over Cuba, he

sent a group of invaders against Panama. On December 1, 1961, in a public speech, he declared himself a Marxist-Leninist and said "I will be so until the day I die." In 1964 the Organization of American States placed sanctions against Castro's Cuba for sending weapons and ammunition to communist guerrillas in Venezuela trying to overthrow the constitutional government of President Romulo Betancourt. In 1965 Castro sheltered and trained one Col. Francisco Caamano and his leftist followers to launch an attack against the Dominican Republic. Caamano was killed in the futile invasion effort near Santo Domingo. In 1969 Castro sponsored the "Venceremos Brigade," a revolutionary organization of Latin Americans in the United States. In 1967 Castro's top lieutenant, Che Guevara, was killed trying to overthrow the government in Bolivia. Cuba's own record condemns it as an aggressor and an enemy of peace.

The evidence is conclusive. Castro is far more than a mere puppet of the Kremlin. He is a major instrument of Moscow's communist military might. Cuba itself is not just a trouble spot, it is the most important trouble source in this hemisphere.

There will be no solution, peaceful or otherwise, in El Salvador or anywhere else in Central America, including, eventually, Mexico, until the core of the spreading communist cancer is cut at its source in Cuba. The United States cannot enjoy peace so long as this communist encirclement to the south continues. And there will be no peace, prosperity, tranquility, serenity, security or true freedom in all of the Americas while Fidel Castro and his communist system and communist allies and communist sponsors — yes, the Soviet Union — remain in power in Cuba.

Castro was trying to act like "Mr. Nice Guy" early in 1982, not because he had become a "soft" communist or because he was changing his policy of militant communist aggression anywhere, but because he feared the U.S. might possibly take advantage of Soviet preoccupation with Afghanistan and Poland to use force against Cuba. Prompted only by fear of U.S. military strength, Castro sent out feelers to Washington indicating he might be willing to play a "positive role" in settling the El Salvador conflict, normalize relations with the U.S., and "talk" about such issues as the Guantanamo Naval Base and the American economic embargo against Cuba.

The taming of Castro was a high-priority objective for the Reagan administration but more is needed than just the settlement of a few side issues as suggested by the Cuban dictator. Cuban troops in Africa must be entirely removed. Cuban-inspired revolt in all of Latin America must be stopped completely. The Cuban sanctuary of Soviet military personnel and weapons must be ended. There is far more to "normalizing" relations with Cuba than Castro seems willing to admit or negotiate. There is little evidence to suggest Castro is going to stop these various activities declared "no longer acceptable" by the American Secretary of State, Alexander Haig, on behalf of President Reagan. More likely, Havana and Washington will continue sparring because, as a major news magazine reported:

"Reagan has made it clear that he shares Haig's conviction that Castro must be stopped. But he has not indicated how he expects to succeed where his six predecessors in the White House failed. Previous administrations have tried in vain to thwart Castro by every conceivable means from an abortive invasion to economic inducements. . . .For the president it could develop into one of the most critical foreign policy decisions he is likely to face in the immediate future."

Chapter 9

THE HARD TRUTH
ABOUT EL SALVADOR

The communists trying to takeover El Salvador have lost on the battlefield and lost at the ballot box but they may win yet because they are winning their propaganda campaign in the American news media and the American Congress — a campaign based on lies!

The biggest of these lies has been that "the people" have supported the communist guerrillas trying to take over the country by force. The next biggest lie is that socialism — misnamed "reform" — is being forced upon the country by its government and U.S. policy is acceptable or popular with most of the people. Lie number 1 is communist. Lie number 2 is of Washington.

Here is what has really happened in El Salvador, and why Salvadorans, while despising the communists, think the United States is two-faced in its policy toward their country:

Although the U.S. free enterprise system is the greatest in the world, the government in Washington is subsidizing a system of state control in El Salvador, most notably the so-called land reform program urged upon that country by President Jimmy Carter, his advisers, and his then ambassador to El Salvador, Robert White. This is the same style of land socialization that has failed in Peru, in Allende's Chile and in Castro's Cuba.

The land socialization system was urged on El Salvador, with a continuance of foreign aid as the bait, to replace a free market economy that was troubled politically but nevertheless doing well enough in such densely populated country whose major resource is land.

Carter mistakenly thought that by taking land away from the land owners of "the right" and re-distributing it to the peasants of "the left" that the threat of Marxism and its proposals for land collectivization could be diminished. Instead, even at the end of Carter's term, he had acknowledged the need for increased military aid against the Marxist guerrillas in El Salvador.

The problem has grown under President Reagan. He has denounced Soviet aid to the guerrillas — something Carter wouldn't admit — but has also increased the foreign aid subsidy for the state-controlled socialist land "reform" system in El Salvador even while calling for government decontrol of the economy in the United States.

The word reform sounds good when broadcast. Reform looks good in print. But the land "reform" in El Salvador is no reform at all. It is a lie to call it reform. It is sheer socialism, through the confiscation and collectivization of land. To divide the small arable area of mountainous El Salvador among the "peasants" would mean those receiving land parcels would get only a few acres — not enough to support a family, especially after a few seasons of intensive agriculture when it would wear out — and several hundred thousand would be left out, getting no land at all. This would cause additional discontent and violence.

When the victorious party leaders from the right met after the 1982 election in an effort to form a coalition and ease out Duarte and his "moderates" or socialists as some see them, U.S. Ambassador Dean Hinton met with them and, in effect, negated the election results by dictating to them the terms under which a coalition could be formed. It would be a coalition including Duarte, a coalition that would not reverse the socialist land and financial "reforms," a coalition that must bow to U.S. dictates from Washington if it wants economic and military aid continued.

One Latin American diplomat said cynically of this deal: "They (Washington) got the election they wanted and they're making sure they get the election results they wanted."

What happened was that when the communists took over Nicaragua in 1979 after Carter had betrayed our long-time ally there, Anastasios Somoza, Carter and his advisers went into a panic over El Salvador, decided to "copycat" Marxism, and encouraged and supported the October 1979 military coup that put the socialist Duarte in power. This new military junta immediately nationalized the overseas marketing of El Salvador's major exports: coffee, cotton and sugar. Then early in 1980 it issued decree number 114 which declared the Salvadoran constitution null and void when it ran counter to the junta's socialization and nationalization efforts.

It was on March 5 and 6, 1980, that the socialist junta supported and directed by Carter seized the private banks and loan institutions and put them under direction of the government. On that same day, squads of soldiers, each accompanied by a Salvadoran land reform institute (ISTA) official, took over 376 of the country's largest and most productive farms and plantations. They took everything — trucks, tractors, houses, personal belongings, business records, crops, fertilizer and seeds.

Not even Castro's seizure of Cuba had been so fast or so thorough. It was a socialist economic blitz the like of which has never been seen in this hemisphere, nor in Mexico, Cuba, Colombia, Bolivia or anywhere.

The whole operation had been planned in advance by Dr. Roy Prosterman, an American working under a U.S. government contract, and the plan has been endorsed by Carter and his diplomats. The land and bank grab was consolidated with help from the American Institute of Free Labor Development under a $1 million U.S. AID contract, AID being a U.S. State Department agency.

The junta announced that land owners would be paid, but contrary to testimony by U.S. government officials before Congress, none have been paid yet. They didn't even get eviction notices. To try to make the land grab look legitimate, the socialist junta instituted retroactive taxes on the land seized and claimed it was taken for non-payment of those taxes, a complete lie.

The socialist junta gave titles to about 100 17-acre plots to make the reform look good on the surface, but most of the confiscated land has been turned into "cooperatives" or communes operated under state direction. Every farmer in El Salvador, whether working on the commune or on the deeded small land tracts, is subject to state direction in what crops to plant, how to manage his business, where and when to market harvests, and also is dependent upon government for agricultural equipment and supplies. Agriculture in El Salvador is being run by the government like the farms in Soviet Russia and Poland.

The land owners, bankers, financiers and middle-class farmers fought back, organizing the right wing parties, some of which supported the "death squads" that have killed land reform officials, including two Americans who were helping direct the collectivization of land in El Salvador.

As the impact of the socialization hit the Salvadoran private sector, thousands of those whose lands and life savings had been taken by the U.S.-supported socialists left the country. They included land owners, managers, technicians, engineers, auditors and later even doctors, pharmacists, bookkeepers, small business owners and shoe clerks as the economy began to weaken. Thus, much of the upper and middle class fled the country and even the peasants began to leave as their employment on the land declined, fleeing over the border into Honduras as the Marxist guerrillas used the socialist-weakened economy as propaganda to promote communism! What irony!

Duarte revealed his socialist sentiments in a Miami, Florida radio interview in March, 1980, saying:

"My government's revolutionary program is much more profound than those presented by the communist party or any leftist party. Our revolutionary process has shattered all the models not only advocated here but in all Latin America. For example, there's not a single country in Latin America where all the foreign commerce and the banking system have been totally nationalized, as in ours. Nor is there a single other country in Latin America, and that includes Cuba, where the wealth that is the land has been given directly to the peasants." (He was talking about the 100 cases made for just such propaganda.)

So Duarte boasted that his government's position was more radical than those of the Salvadoran Marxist-Leninist forces!

So the U.S. taxpayer is stuck with subsidizing an unpopular socialist regime in El Salvador.

The long-range plan for U.S. economic and military aid to the socialist government of Duarte in El Salvador was estimated at $1 billion over the next five years, should it last that long. More than $200 million has been spent on it since 1979.

But the land socialization program is doomed to failure no matter how much U.S. aid is squandered on it. History tells us that. Mexico's experience with nearly 70 years of socialized land reform, Peru's with 12 recent years, Chile's under Allende, Argentina's under Peron's export-control system, and the heavily-subsidized Cuban revolution under two decades of Soviet sponsorship have all failed miserably.

In El Salvador, sugar exports have practically come to a halt. Closed, burned or terribly mismanaged sugar mills dot the countryside. Sugar provided the third largest source of foreign exchange in El Salvador before the socialization program. Cotton production is down by 35 per cent. The government lost $40 million marketing recent coffee crops.

The land socialization in El Salvador was based on a phony legend that the 8,000 square mile country, about the size of Connecticut, was controlled by "14 families" and their corrupt military, both dedicated to grinding down the poor. But income tax rolls showed that there were in fact more than 30,000 people in the nation of 4 million who were in the highest income bracket. It also should be noted that before the socialization, El Salvador was self-sufficient in food, something Mexico has not achieved in its years of revolutionary land reform.

The news media has failed or ignored a story about statistics from the World Bank, Inter-American Development Bank and United Nations showing that El Salvador compared favorably with other Latin American nations in social programs before the land and money grab. In 1977, for example, El Salvador spent 32 per cent of its government expenditures on social programs, compared with 18.5 per cent by Mexico and 18.8 per cent by oil-rich and liberal Venezuela.

The same figures show that there was a dramatic redistribution of income going on in El Salvador under the free market system between 1965 and 1977. Most of the redistribution benefited "the lower 40 per cent of the people," according to the World Bank.

The United Nations, in that same period, reported that El Salvador's concentration of wealth was more moderate than such countries as Argentina, Chile and Venezuela, and that statistics on infant mortality and nutritional deficiency were not out of line with other Latin American nations.

But the news media, communist propaganda, speakers in the U.S. Congress, and a variety of clergymen, educators and others supposedly knowledgeable about El Salvador simply avoid all these facts and make no mention of the land theft and bank and financial grab made by the socialists first supported by Jimmy Carter and later endorsed by Ronald Reagan.

If the United States truly wants to save El Salvador from communism, it will continue its economic and military aid and it will abandon the Jimmy Carter land and bank nationalization schemes that have done far more to wreck the economy than the communist guerrillas have done.

The communists will continue their drive for conquest in El Salvador and the rest of Central America to cut the hemisphere in two at the waist, to drive on through Guatemala and take the oil fields of southern Mexico, and to probe northward toward Texas to test what resistance, if any, there is before reaching the Rio Grande.

The encirclement of America from the south was almost invited by the weak-spined administration of Jimmy Carter who betrayed Somoza and socialized the economy in El Salvador in a futile attempt to appease communism with watered-down communistic efforts instead of military strength based on a strong free enterprise economy.

American congressional liberals and the Marxist-oriented governments of Mexico, Venezuela and Panama continue to seek some kind of negotiated settlement with the communist guerrillas in El Salvador and their sponsors and suppliers in Nicaragua, Cuba and the Soviet Union.

There is no way to negotiate with communists. They don't want negotiation. They want total surrender. They are not negotiators anyway . . . they are gangsters. They don't represent anyone but themselves. They never won any election anywhere. Who do they think they are? Who does Congress think they are? The only way to resist the international gangsters, communists who would force their way into government without benefit of a legal democratic election is, unfortunately, with force.

It is they who force the choice upon us: *surrender or fight.*

Boiled down, that's the story of El Salvador and the fight against communism everywhere.

Central America is too small a place to contain the fighting in a small country like El Salvador, which is about the size of Connecticut or the northeast quarter of Oklahoma. That's why the war has spilled over into Honduras and Guatemala and Nicaragua . . . and even sparked terrorist actions in peaceful little Costa Rica. That's why refugees are streaming out of the little Central American countries into Mexico, and why many Mexicans are getting more and more restless — both economically and politically as the pressure of communism spreads — and are entering the United States in ever increasing numbers, beating the rush.

For the rush is coming for certain to the Southwest United States if El Salvador falls to communism. The pattern is already set by the immigrant flow . . . into Guatemala and Honduras, into Mexico, into Texas and Southern California, New Mexico and Arizona.

This fight against communism is not overseas in Vietnam or Korea anymore. It is here on our doorstep. There is no ocean between us and El Salvador, only Guatemala and Mexico and the Rio Grande River. Where are we going to resist? In the streets of Phoenix and Los Angeles and San Antonio? Or are we going to fight at all? Congress wants to withdraw military aid to El Salvador and surrender. But even that won't stop it. Guatemala's next, then Mexico, then Texas. Somewhere we have to make a choice and make a stand.

Fidel Castro was interviewed by a correspondent for a radio station broadcasting from Colombia, South America, and here is his message to America:

"The United States must first persuade itself that it is losing the war in El Salvador, that it is losing the land."

Castro went on to say that he was pleased to see that the news media and the Congress in the United States were *"resisting"* — as he put it — *"resisting" President Reagan's policy* of supporting the El Salvador government and implementing the Caribbean Basin Initiative plan for economic development in the area.

The communist violence in El Salvador breaks out every six months shortly before Congress must certify some advance in human rights and authorize continuing military aid to the democratic government of El Salvador. This communist trouble is timed to try to persuade Congress that the government of El Salvador is "losing" the war and control of the land. The leftist, liberal national news media have been trying to convince American television viewers and newspaper and news magazine readers of that for years . . . even without Castro's help.

But before Castro and Congress and the news media convince us the war in El Salvador is lost, let's look at the facts. The facts are that the **communist guerrillas** in El Salvador **are the ones who are losing.** Oh, they make headlines and TV film footage by shooting up some small mountain town every once in a while and holding it for a few hours, then ambushing the relief column, but the fact is that they do not control any one of El Salvador's 32 government provinces — like counties or states in America — either militarily or economically.

Here is another fact that communist-favoring American news media ignored. There was a big demonstration, a parade, downtown in the capital of El Salvador protesting AGAINST any government negotiations with the communists. Our TV people chose not to report that demonstration but if it had been a communist demonstration favoring negotiations it would have been reported. The fact is that the communists no longer are strong enough to mount demonstrations in the capital or any other important city in El Salvador.

Here is another fact unreported in the news media. Congressman Phil Crane visited El Salvador and talked not only with officials but with people in the street, the market place and on buses. He said this upon his return to the U.S., and I quote him:

"From no individual did I hear either 'sympathy for the communist guerrillas nor interest in negotiating with them unless they were willing to lay down their arms and work within the democratic system."

In the Gulf of Fonesca, between El Salvador and Nicaragua, the Salvadoran Navy with U.S. equipment has drastically cut down the supply of arms reaching the guerrillas by sea from Nicaragua. The overland mountain trails are also being cut off frequently by government forces. The problem is an air lift of supplies. Nicaragua flies arms and supplies to the guerrillas in small planes, landing on tiny dirt strips in cotton fields and cleared areas in coffee plantations to unload supplies. The Salvadoran Air Force, consisting of 19 U.S. helicopters, desperately needs more air defense, spare parts and training, to cut off the aerial supply of the guerrillas

If the U.S. doesn't continue to assist El Salvador resist communist guerrilla aggression, then it will be a clear message back to Castro and his Moscow masters that the United States of America is no longer interested in protecting democracy in the Western Hemisphere, even close to home. Did you know that Miami, Florida is closer to El Salvador than it is to Washington D.C.?

Cuba and the Soviet Union will continue to press communist subversion and armed insurrection at every opportunity, especially if Congress and the news media ever persuade the American people — as Castro suggests — that the war in El Salvador is lost. It isn't lost and it won't be as long as we stand by our friends fighting for freedom that's closer to Miami than Miami is to Washington.

While the Pope s visit to Central America drew a lot of attention to that area, the news media covering it conveniently left out a big story that told the truth about the **Marxist murderers** in El Salvador.

Some time ago the Marxists took over a little town called Berlin in El Salvador. Not Berlin, Germany, but a little place with the same name . . . Berlin in El Salvador. That's where an American soldier was wounded while observing the action from a helicopter.

Well, while the news media concentrated on the Pope they

brushed aside the following investigative report released by the Human Rights Commission of El Salvador about what really happened when the Marxist guerrillas took over that little town.

1. They indiscriminately **attacked the civilian population,** causing fires, looting stores and homes and offices, running off several thousand people from their homes.

2. The town was attacked for the **loot.** It was not a military target. There were only 43 policemen and national guardsmen on duty there when the Marxists struck.

3. The civilians remaining in the town were **forced at gunpoint** to go to a city park and participate in a **televised demonstration** supposedly celebrating the communist victory. This kind of propaganda psychology was shown on American television with the distinct purpose of convincing the American people and their Congressmen that the communists were winning in Central America when that is not the truth. This was just one little isolated village in a remote mountain area but American TV made it look like a demonstration in New York's Central Park.

4. The guerrillas caused the deaths of at least 12 **defenseless civilians,** including women, children and elderly people.

Where were the television cameras when these helpless and innocent people were being buried? If they had been killed by government troops or state police the cameras would have been everywhere. But the big American television networks didn't see fit to film the **victims of communist cruelty and barbarism.**

Why didn't the TV cameras take some footage of the vandalism, looting and theft that happened in that village, all done by the communists who were only there long enough to loot and murder and film what they claimed was a victory?

The real heartbreak is still with that little town. The courageous people there who have told the truth about the attack now go **ignored by the big news media** and the American Congress that seems to think that only the communists are good in El Salvador and everyone else there, the government and general population both, are bad.

It is distressing to see America turn defeatist about El Salvador because of the news media and a Congress that **refuse to face the truth** about what is really happening there and are willing to settle for communist propaganda instead.

Let's get a couple of things straight about El Salvador and the rest of Latin America that the leftist, liberal national news media distorts, misunderstands or deliberately lies about in its reporting:

1. The guerrillas fighting the legitimate government in El Salvador are not insurgents or leftists, they are out and out communists. The guerrilla war that they have been conducting in El Salvador is the classic Communist style of warfare as planned by Lenin, Mao Tse-Tung, and Fidel Castro and his helper, Che Guevara . . . all of them 100 per cent dedicated communists.

2. The news media reporting of any election in El Salvador or any other country threatened by communist revolution is going to be slanted in favor of the communists because it is controversy that makes news, not peaceful progress or due process of law. The elections in El Salvador have been no worse than some we have seen in this country in Cook County, Illinois, or Washington, D.C., or Jersey City, New Jersey, or Boston, Massachusetts, when it comes to corruption.

3. The misnamed "land reform" programs that have been instituted in El Salvador are not really land reforms at all but communist programs for taking land from one group of people by force and distributing it to others who are in political accord with the takers. In other words, the misnamed land reform that was begun during the Carter administration under the direction of then ambassador Robert White and then Salvadoran President Jose Napoleon Duarte is nothing more than the same kind of communist land seizure that was carried out in Nicaragua by the Sandinista communists. The Carter land reform in El Salvador was and even today continues to be an *appeasement to communism*, the seizure of coffee and sugar plantations, banks and export business from private enterprise owners, capitalist owners, and turning them over to communists and to government bureaucratic managers who are communist sympathizers. It really is that simple, believe it or not!

The national news media that reports on El Salvador refuses to report that. The news media didn't report the truth about the loss of China or Cuba or Nicaragua and is not reporting the truth about the almost certain loss of El Salvador to communism unless the American people and the representatives they send to Congress wake up to the facts of communism and decide to support freedom instead of communism in El Salvador and the rest of Latin America.

4. The biased news media has been trying to blame most of the deaths in El Salvador on what they call "right wing death squads" but there would be no such thing if there were no communist invaders in El Salvador. The private army the American press calls death squads is fighting against both the

communists and the communist appeasement in land redistribution, banking and exporting that the Carter administration *imposed* on El Salvador and that the Reagan administration has been unable to *undo* because of Congress.

Now, what I'm going to say is not a popular thing to say but it must be said: the only effective force fighting communism in El Salvador today is the private army of the free enterprise capitalists who are having their land, their money and their business taken away from them by communist force and by communist injustice. The American leftist, liberal national news media calls that army "death squads," a marvelous propaganda trick.

But the truth is that *that army* is the only one effective against the communists. The government army, with all the military supplies and helicopters and advisers the United States has provided it, is still ineffective, still suffering defeat after defeat, and still projecting a losing image because it hasn't the same reason to fight as the imdependent army fighting communism for both tangible and spiritual reasons.

To my knowledge, Christian Crusade is the only source in America reporting this side of the story. The rest of them have *bought the communist line* of how to report on El Salvador, which is the same way they reported on China, Cuba and Nicaragua.

IN CONCLUSION

Communism is encircling the United States with the point of its sickle now stabbed into the heart of Central America and its hammer ready to pound it through Mexico into the soft underbelly of the United States.

The communists are pinching off the "narrow waist" that connects North and South America by taking over Central America with armed force. They are winning there because America is afraid — not only afraid to fight but even afraid to help our friends who are fighting for survival. America has been afraid to fight since Korea and especially since Vietnam.

What America is afraid of is nuclear warfare. Because of that fear we have been giving up our former friends in the free world to communism, country by country, crisis by crisis.

America is afraid because too many Americans and too many of their once-cherished institutions have turned their back on God and lost their faith in God, their once-vaunted trust in God to protect us.

There is only one way to stop the rising Red tide from finally overwhelming us and that is to turn back to God instead of turning our back to Him. We must repent from what have become nationally sinful ways, seek God's forgiveness, and ask again for His help and protection.

Spiritually, we must reevaluate and reestablish our priorities to put God first in our national life and such things as commerce, politics and finances in appropriate secondary positions. Then God will hear our cry and heal our land, just as it says in II Coronicles 7:14.

When we get ourselves right with God spiritually in America, then He will provide the means in leadership and resources to take an entirely new course to save ourselves from our enemies, the godless communists.

God intends for us to defend ourselves and our loved ones from those who would enslave us. This is clear in I Timothy 5:8: *"But if any provide not for his own, and specially for those of his own house, he hath denied the faith, and is worse than an infidel."*

If we have our national house in order and have a national faith in God, then He will see us through present and future dangers and enable us to defend ourselves. And if we fail, we will be worse than the infidels of communism and being worse will serve them as slaves.

With renewed spiritual strength from God, America can develop a strong and decisive physical foreign policy based on military strength that will have as its main purpose the development of a world alliance of free and God-loving nations shaped, to the largest degree possible, with our national interests at heart. And if our national interests are shaped by God and righteousness, then such a policy would be in God's will and be successful.

Our nation is and has been historically that of a great world power that is unashamedly free, democratic and capitalistic.

Unless we develop this course of action soon we will be completely encircled and engulfed by communism because we will have forfeited freedom, democracy and capitalism. When that happens, America will fall without a very good fight, maybe with no fight at all, like the proverbial plum right into the communists' hands, just as Lenin predicted 60 years ago.

We have seen England, once the Christian leader of the free world, become a third or fourth rate power because it too often failed to exercise its military might in peacetime, the Falklands notwithstanding. America will lose its place as the free world leader and become a second — or third, fourth or fifth — rate power for the same reason if it doesn't change course immediately to stand firm against godless communism that has never wavered in its aim to enslave us.

Winston Churchill was talking about England in the 1930s but he might as well have been talking about America and its timid little Congresses of recent times when he said:

"Virtuous motives, trammeled by intertia and timidity, are no match for armed and resolute wickedness. A sincere love of peace is no excuse for muddling hundreds of millions of people

*into total war. The cheers of the weak, well-meaning
assemblies soon cease to echo, and their votes soon cease to
count. Doom marches on.*"

Millions of people died around the globe in World War II
because those who wanted peace at almost any price failed to
pay attention to such warnings as Churchill's.

Now the same thing is happening again with a ruthless
tyranny, communism, threatening free and peace-loving
nations just as the Axis did before and during World War II.
The Soviet Union and its communist stooges and proxies are
marching on like the doom that Churchill mentioned. This was
seen clearly enough at the outset of the Korean War when then
Secretary of State George C. Marshall said:

*"We have tried since the birth of our nation to promote our
love of peace by a display of weakness. This course has failed
utterly."*

And yet we continue to try it.

**The immediate threat to American geographical security
today is coming through Central America and through Soviet
military power.**

If we fail to help and to hold El Salvador, for example, the
communists will move on to Mexico. They don't really care
much for El Salvador but they must have it to secure the
Central American base for their drive to take the oil fields of
Southern Mexico, their immediate goal in Central America. It
is only 10 hours drive by tank to Texas from El Salvador and
only two hours flight by jet plane from there to Houston, New
Orleans or Miami.

We are faced by a godless, ruthless power in communism
that cares nothing for moral values, honorable contracts,
solemn treaties or negotiated and agreed upon terms. Such a
power can only be opposed successfully by a stronger power,
the power of God over the power of Satan.

Americans have been misled by uninformed or unscrupulous
politicians, and by a leftist, liberal national news media that
has failed to report all the important facts, to believe that
"power politics" is un-American because it is immoral, and
that the use of force ought to be replaced by the rule of
international law in the form of a supergovernment such as the
United Nations. They have advised compromise and
accommodation with our enemies in the name of sweet
reasonableness and mislabeled "love." It was this kind of
"make love, not war" attitude that was largely responsible for
forfeit and needless loss in Vietnam. Christian love is not the
kind of love for humanity and mankind that would surrender

all to Satan at any cost rather than stand up for what is right.

The cowards, the phony pacifists, the utopians, the liberal intellectuals, the dreamers and the deceivers have created an illusion through the news media and in Washington that the rest of the world will love and admire America for being peaceful and for doing nice things for them.

But the fact is that many, many nations hate us for what we really are: free, democratic, capitalist. These anti-American nations — and no amount of foreign aid will ever change their minds — are more interested in what they might DO TO US than in what we might DO FOR THEM. And those few "neutral" or so-called "non-aligned Third World" nations that don't openly hate us could never be reliable friends and allies unless they respect us and even fear us to some extent.

The battle for the "hearts and minds" of mankind now going on between godless communism and the remaining free nations of the world IS World War III. It will be won by the strong in heart and in mind and in soul — and in military stature — not by those whose idea of winning a fight is to stage a cost-efficient public relations compaign. That's why we lost in Vietnam, not on the battlefield itself but in the political arena because our leadership did not have the will of strong hearts, minds and souls to win.

Communism's relentless drive for world conquest has led to the greatest extremes known to man. It has killed 142 million people since the Russian Revolution in 1917 and the toll mounts daily in such places as El Salvador and Afghanistan.

About 70 million Russians have been liquidated by their communist masters, about 66 million Chinese, and some 6 million plus in communist revolutions, insurrections, terrorist acts and misrule elsewhere in the world. These figures have been compiled through United Nations reports, Amnesty International, the London Daily Telegraph special report on communist genocide dated April 24, 1979, and various other documents.

Genocide has been a way of life and death in both Russian and communist history. What might be called "modern" Russian history dates from the cruelties of Ivan the Terrible, just as the permanent settlement of the Plymouth Rock pilgrims dates the approximate beginning of traditional American history. The two nations that are now superpowers of the world have been on a virtually inevitable collision course with those disparate backgrounds — one, the Russian-Soviet nation steeped in blood and violence and tyranny and godlessness; the other, a basically Christian nation with a Biblical foundation and a history of religious tolerance for more than two centuries.

Now we are approaching the climax of this great confrontation, this struggle between the earthly representatives of good and evil, of God and Satan. The communist evil is not national, it is not "Russian" but it is international and Russia was its first victim.

The nations that fall to communism cease to exist as nations except on the map and in historical reference. They may be called Poland or Afghanistan or El Salvador or Nicaragua or Ethiopia but under communism they have lost all national identity.

They have simply become part of the international communist organization that controls all it takes. There no longer really is a Russia or a China. The two communist parties that control those places may have doctrinal and factional differences but they are nevertheless communist and will stand together when challenged or, should it become absolutely necessary, unite in order to continue world conquest rather than give it up. America's political leadership in recent years simply cannot understand this and continues to be deluded by trying to deal separately with communists of the international organization purporting to represent nations that no longer exist. They may be identified ethnically as Russians or Chinese but they don't consider themselves as such and are in heart, mind and godless soul, communists. The communist minority rules the majority of their countrymen by force, having taken political control by violence in all cases rather than by any democratic or popular process.

Communism is imposed on a nation from the top down, not by a popular "grassroots revolution" from the bottom up as communist propagandists would have the rest of the world believe. Nowhere, and certainly not in Russia or China, the two largest countries taken over by communism, have "the people" installed a communist government by peaceful means nor has one tested its political popularity among "the people" by the electoral process unless that election was completely controlled by the force of the communist state and staged as a propaganda vehicle.

Communism is socialism carried to an extremely centralized control and carried on at an international level. It means the nationalization of industry and communications, the collectivization of agriculture, the banishment of any true religious worship with only state controlled or approved churches allowed to remain open, and the management of the economy by political means enforced by military strength. Socialism, such as Hitler's national socialist state, is communism on merely a national scale. Contrary to what the news media and academicians and intellectuals and others have claimed, the fascism of Hitler's socialist state and the communism of Stalin's socialist state did not represent a "right" and a "left" in the political spectrum but were both far left socialist political movements with Soviet communism moving on to an international scale during and after World War II.

We should not forget during the ebb and flow of "peaceful co-existence" and "detente" and all other compromises and appeasements with the communists, that they are, after all, atheists. The Soviet Communist Party in the early 1980s began a new campaign to intensify and "modernize" atheist education. In the process, it intensified persecution of all religions within its power, especially Christianity. One report on this new Soviet fight against God said:

"One of the fundamental objectives of the Soviet state is to supplant religious faith with the ideals, values and world view encapsulated in Lenin's version of Marxist ideology, which itself has assumed the character of a competing but secular religion, even to the extent of imitating practices of the Russian Orthodox Church."

The world is faced with the same extreme socialist evil we thought was defeated in World War II, only today it is on a much broader international scale. Through communism, Satan has risen from the ashes of World War II to become a greater threat than ever to God's peaceful and freedom loving people. And it is to God whom they must turn for protection and for victory.

Only with His blessing will God's people be triumphant in this greatest test yet of good versus evil on the face of the earth. America has been blessed by God since its founding because it was founded like no other nation on earth — on God's principles set out in His Holy Word. The attacks today from many sources on God and His Word are doing their best to undermine this great country.

Already weakened to some considerable extent from within, the United States of America now faces the greatest threat to its existence yet by the communist encirclement closing in on its borders with vice-like strength. Whether we crack under all these pressures or break their power is the issue that will decide the fate of the world as we know it. That's what this book is all about.

In II Chronicles 7:14, there is a key to survival — to holding back the forces of anti-christ communism:

"If my people, which are called by my name shall humble themselves, and pray, and seek my face, and turn from their wicked ways; then I will hear from heaven, and will for give their sin, and will heal their land."

POSTSCRIPT TO CHRISTIANS

Almost forty years ago, as a young pastor, I felt led of the Lord to devote my entire life standing "for Christ and against Satan." I accepted the commandment of God in Ezekiel 33:7 as my "marching orders": "*So thou, O son of man, I have set thee to be a watchman under the house of . . . God; therefore thou shall hear the word at My mouth, and warn the people for me.*"

I have been on daily network radio on a program called "Christian Crusade" for nearly forty years and have been on national television even a year longer than that. It has not been easy. However, in time I grew accustomed to the attacks from the pro-Communist Americans news media and the liberal elements of the clergy, education, politics, etc. I frankly confess a continued sense of disappointment that I have been unable to do more for "God and Country" because of my failure to raise sufficient amounts of money to underwrite a more effective worldwide crusade against Communism.

The Bible warns us that in the end-time, so-called Christians will "not listen to sound doctrine. . . but will heep to themselves teachers, having itching ears." (II Timothy 4:3) In other words, the time will come and indeed has arrived, when a majority of God's people no longer want to hear their preachers and priests preaching God's prophetic warnings, repentance and Christian holiness. Instead, they want to be entertained from the pulpit. They want to be told that it doesn't make any difference what they believe or how one lives their daily lives since God is not interested in our personal beliefs or our damning sins. On the basis of God's Word, I know that we will spend eternity in Hell if we die believing that we can live like the devil and still be a part of God's promised rapture of the Church . . . the Second Coming of Christ.

In I Thessalonians 4:16-17: *"For the Lord Himself shall descend from heaven with a shout . . . we which are alive and remain shall be caught up together (or raptured) . . . in the clouds to meet the Lord in the air: and so shall we ever be with the Lord."*

However, the Rapture is for blood-bought saints washed in the blood of the Lamb, obedient to the commandments of Christ. The Rapture is to allow all Christian believers, "both living and dead", who kept the faith and even suffered persecution and hardship for their stand for God and the Gospel of Jesus Christ, to escape the seven-year reign of Satan on earth during the Tribulation Period which has been brought about by a satanic world Communist revolution.

Make no mistake about it. The Communists are winning. Hitler died; Nazism died with him. Mussolini died; Fascism died with him. Tojo died; Japanese militarism died with him. Stalin is dead; COMMUNISM LIVES ON. Lenin is dead; COMMUNISM LIVES ON. Mao is dead; COMMUNISM LIVES ON. Why? Because Communism is a *satanic* weapon more powerful than the atom bomb, hydrogen bomb, cobalt bomb, or all of them combined, to bring about the seven-year Tribulation Period in which the whole world will worship Satan and his son, the anit-Christ, who will be the leader of a godless world government, and his religious counter-part, the "false prophet," the false Messiah.

I can hear someone say, *"As a Christian, I reject that kind of talk. Christians should not get involved in 'politics.' What you are saying doesn't reflect* **any** *faith."* Friend, if this is the way you feel, your problem is that you don't know the Word of God . . . the Bible. You don't know what Bible prophecy teaches. If you did, you would know the world is to get worse before the ultimate reign of Christ upon the earth as King of Kings and Lord of Lords. There must be a seven-year Tribulation Period during which Satan and anti-Christ rules over the earth.

Now the Bible doesn't teach that *all* Americans will be raptured and will escape the Tribulation Period. In fact, Jesus once said, *"Not every one that saith unto me, Lord, shall enter the Kingdom of Heaven, but he that doeth the will of my Father which is in Heaven. . ."* (Matthew 7:21) The Rapture is a supernatural way of escaping for true Christians who believed in the miraculous death, burial and resurrection of Christ and faithfully kept His commandments such as supporting causes like Christian Crusade who for forty years has held back the forces of anti-Christ Communism with the use of mass world communications. In other words, the Rapture will be for those believers who took Jesus' commandments and prophetic warnings seriously and were truly involved in holding back the forces of anti-Christ in the immoral world in which they lived.

Most Christians in America won't even associate with a man like Billy James Hargis or a movement like Christian Crusade. After all, the atheists and pro-Communist elements in high places in America have branded people like me extremist and radical, and who would want to be friendly to someone like that? As a result, frankly, we have not been able to raise the money in recent years to do all that we were capable of doing for Christ and against Communism . . . for good and against evil . . . for God and against Satan.

We live in a time when people are looking for those "teachers . . . having itching ears." They want to be entertained from the pulpit. They like the so-called "prosperity preachers" or "positive thinking motivators" in the pulpit who preach their soft gospels, promising riches and peace to everyone. Such men dominate the religious airwaves. Some are on a thousand radio and television stations but let a man like Billy James Hargis come along with God's message of end-time truth, urging Americans to repent, get right with God and prepare for the Rapture as the only way out for us, and his warning often falls on deaf ears.

Brethren, I would be afraid to meet God in Judgment after having spurned this message of calling America to repentance and sounding the trumpet of warning concerning the coming Communist-initiated Tribulation Period and the even-sooner coming of Jesus Christ to rapture the Christians and take us out of this sin-dominated world.

I can hear someone say, "*Well, if all of this is prophesied in the Bible, why should I support a cause to try to stop it?*" May I remind you of two Scriptures that will answer your question. Jesus said to Judas as He sat by him at the Last Supper: "*Woe be unto that man by whom the Son of man is betrayed. . . .*" (Matthew 26:24) In other words, it was true that the Old Testament prophesied that Judas would betray Jesus Christ for thirty pieces of silver but God have mercy on Judas for his sin and betrayal of the Lord. To apply that to our day, it is true that the world will get worse and worse necessitating the coming of Christ to rapture the Christians out of the world, but woe be unto those Christians that never gave of themselves *or their means* to help hold back the forces of anti-Christ Communism, thus allowing the peoples of the Free World a few more decades to separate themselves from the things of the world and join the King of Kings in His plan of redemption.

The other Scripture that I was thinking about is in Luke 19:13 when Jesus said simply: *"Occupy til I come. . ."* We are like sentries on a military post — we are to occupy until He returns. We will answer to God for our failure to stand up and be counted "for Christ and against Communism." Christian Crusade offered us a chance to do something about reaching the world by the use of mass communication "for Christ and against Communism." Our failure to support it is an act of disobedience that God is surely mindful of.

I urge you as long as we have a year of freedom, let's fight for God and country. I urge you to join Christian Crusade by supporting each month this ministry so that we can print more books like this, buy more radio and TV time and get our message out to the masses. Brethren, it's the end-time. Judgment is ahead. We must repent of our sin. We must get right with God. We must support the right causes. Each of us should be a consecutive giver to this nonprofit "Christian Crusade (Billy James Hargis Evangelistic Association, Inc.)" as an obedient child of God determined to do our best until Christ raptures us out of this sin-cursed and Communist-dominated world.

A portion of your tithe of your income sent to Christian Crusade would probably go further towards holding back evil, allowing souls to be won to Christ by Godly ministers across the land, than we would ever imagine. We should pledge something every month. We should be a consecutive giver. We should share a portion of our tithes with Christian Crusade. God expects it. Duty demands it. America needs it. Write Christian Crusade, P.O. Box 977, Tulsa, Oklahoma 74102, and a pledge of prayer from you will be equally appreciated.

I have finished writing a follow-up to this book: "COMMUNIST AMERICA: MUST IT BE?". . . AN UPDATE. My new book gives additional revealing and sobering information that is not found in this book about the encirclement of the United States by Communists and the *internal threat* of Communism within our own country. Pray that God will enable us to rush this book into print soon through the generosity of Christians.

Billy James Hargis, D.D., L.L.D
Post Office Box 977
Tulsa, Oklahoma 74102